what is your clutter costing you?

Praise for

what is your clutter costing you?

"Robyn begins her book with a personal invitation to explore the impact clutter has on the quality of your life. She shares her go-to mantra, 'Everything has a price—time, space, money, or energy,' and then digs into this in her powerful and thoughtful book on bringing peace to your life through organization. If clutter is weighing you down, you'll feel much better after reading this book!"

—**ELLEN FAYE,** PCC, CPLC, CPO®, certified productivity leadership coach, former president of the National Association of Productivity and Organizing Professionals (NAPO)

"I have known Robyn for over twenty-five years. Can categorically state that I have never met a force of nature quite like Robyn! She simply gets things done, gets them done efficiently, and takes names later! I often state: 'Robyn has made me what I am today... exhausted!' "

—**MICHAEL KARLIN,** founding partner of NSKFB

"Robyn Reynolds is a unique professional organizer, so it's no surprise her latest book has a unique message: all things are energy. Her talent is harnessing the energy of things, people, and spaces. *What Is Your Clutter Costing You?* is very refreshing, especially for those challenged by disorganization."

—**JUDITH KOLBERG,** organizing industry thought leader and book coach

what is your clutter costing you?

How You're Paying for Clutter,
Even If You Already Own It

by

Robyn Reynolds

Books That Save Lives

Published by Books That Save Lives, an imprint of Jim Dandy, Publishing, LLC

Cover, Layout & Design: Megan Werner
Illustration: Yanka / stock.adobe.com

Jim Dandy Publishing
6252 Peach Avenue
Van Nuys, CA 91411

info@jimdandypublishing.com

For bulk orders, special quantities, course adoptions, and corporate sales, please email info@jimdandypublishing.com

What Is Your Clutter Costing You? How You're Paying for Clutter, Even If You Already Own It

Library of Congress Cataloging-in-Publication number: 2025931389
ISBN: (p) 978-1-68481-824-2 (e) 978-1-68481-825-9
BISAC category code: HOM019000 HOUSE & HOME / Cleaning, Caretaking & Organizing

Printed in the United States of America

Names of clients have been changed to protect the identity and privacy of those depicted.

This book is dedicated to my daughter Kennedy. You are my light and my inspiration for everything I do. Thank you for being the kind, genuine soul that you are.

contents

a personal invitation

"Organizing is a journey, not a destination."

—UNKNOWN

For well over a decade, I have worked in my own business as a professional organizer. When people hear the term "professional organizer," they often have varied ideas of what it means. I get everything from a political organizer to an event organizer to someone who simply arranges items neatly or tidies up rooms.

The reality is the role of a professional organizer is much more complex. As a certified professional organizer, I am, in essence, a problem solver. I like to say that I find space where there seemingly is none while implementing systems that bring order and efficiency to chaotic environments. Not to mention there is a huge psychological component to the work because people have emotional attachments to their belongings.

The work of a professional organizer goes far beyond mere tidying. It involves understanding the unique challenges and needs of each client and creating tailored solutions that address their specific issues. This requires a keen eye for detail, a creative mind to envision potential uses of space, and a strategic approach to ensure that the solutions are sustainable in the long term.

I know firsthand how many people struggle with clutter in their homes. The accumulation of items can happen so subtly that before you know it, your living space feels cramped and overwhelming. Clutter can affect all aspects of life, from physical comfort and safety to mental health and overall well-being. This is where my expertise comes into play. I've dedicated my career to helping individuals and families reclaim their living spaces from the chaos of clutter, while transforming their homes into organized, functional, and serene environments. Through my work, I have seen the profound impact that a well-organized space can have on a person's life.

According to Dictionary.com, clutter is defined as "a disorderly heap or assemblage" or "a state or condition of confusion." Over the years, there is one particular phrase I find myself repeating over and over. I don't even remember when I first started saying it. The phrase has almost become a mantra for me, somewhat of a guiding principle for both my clients and me. The saying is, "Everything has a price—time, space, money, or energy." I tend to use this phrase when my clients are challenged in letting go of some of their items.

This "mantra" came to me one day, almost as if a lightbulb flickered on in my mind. Since then, I've witnessed the profound impact it has on my clients. When I share this phrase, clients regularly stop and really take the time to think about what I've just said and how it might relate to them. That moment of reflection is exactly what I aim for. I want my clients and you to realize the multifaceted impact that clutter can have on your life. Clutter isn't just a physical inconvenience; it's an emotional, financial, and mental drain. My intention with this book is to help you become aware of the hidden costs of clutter, costs that you may never have considered before. Is your clutter costing you time? Space? Money? Or energy? It might be one of these, more than one, or even all of them.

My hope is that once you are aware of these costs, you might be inspired to change your habits. People often think that organizing is only about putting a square peg in a round hole. Newsflash: I'm here to tell you it is so much more than that. Organizing is a very interesting concept. On the one hand, it seems like it should be really easy to be organized. It's something that everyone should be able to do, right? After all, it's not rocket science or brain surgery, is it? But if it's so simple, why do so many people struggle with being organized? Why is it such a challenge for so many to manage and maintain their clutter? The truth is organizing is not as simple as it seems. It's not that cut-and-dry.

When you are challenged by disorganization and have no idea how to get your clutter under control, you sometimes find yourself stuck, like a deer in headlights, or just plain paralyzed and not sure about how to move forward. Why is that? The reason is because the ability to organize is actually a brain-based skill. We all have things that we are good at, and we all have things that are a challenge. While you may struggle with organizing, I struggle with technology. No matter how much you talk to me about gigs and bytes or rams, it just doesn't sink into my brain. We all have our unique strengths and challenges. You should no longer beat yourself up if it isn't easy for you to get organized, because now you know why: it's how your brain is wired. Understanding that your difficulty with organizing is not a personal failing can be truly liberating.

I say all this because I want you to understand the price of what your clutter is costing you. Please don't feel bad, and do not let anyone else make you feel bad about it either. Just know you can always make changes. You can learn to do it yourself or you can hire a professional to help you. The journey to a clutter-free life is about understanding, patience, and the willingness to take that first step. So, let's dive in and explore the cost of your clutter.

As we embark on this journey together, I will share stories from my own experiences as a certified professional organizer. You'll hear about my philosophy when it comes to organizing, and you'll also hear about some of the challenges my clients have faced. Together, we'll uncover the true cost of your clutter—at any rate, that is our goal. Let's begin.

time

"Until we can manage time,
we can manage nothing else."

—PETER DRUCKER

What exactly is time? According to Merriam-Webster, time is defined as "the measured or measurable period during which an action, process, or condition exists or continues." But what does that actually mean? I interpret this to mean that time is something that occurs at a certain period or over a designated period. For instance, school starts at eight in the morning. This is something that occurs at a certain period. A game that takes place between 5–7 p.m. is something that occurs over a designated period. With that being said, I also understand time to be either stagnant or active. It may sound odd but is in fact very true. Stagnant time would be considered a specified moment, such as seeing the time on a digital clock. Active time would be considered as movement. To illustrate this, active time would be seeing the hands on an analog clock moving from one minute to the next. When it comes to how this relates to clutter —bear with me, because this is very important—in the analog clock example, you are actually witnessing the passage of time. This is because you can literally see the hands of the clock moving.

Seeing time passing one minute to the next allows you to gauge how long it will take for you to do something, or how much time you are using, as well as how much time you have left. However, now that we live in a digital world, learning to tell time on an analog clock, as we used to do as young students in grade school, isn't as much of a priority. While they do continue to teach children how to tell time on an analog clock, there is very little "time" spent on the topic. No pun intended. Those of you with kids know what I'm talking about.

Let me tell you a funny story about telling time. When my daughter was in high school, she couldn't tell time on an analog clock. She would probably disagree, but to me being able to tell time means looking at the clock and instantly knowing what time it is. She would be able to figure out the time on an analog clock, but she would actually have to figure it out by figuring out which hand was where and so on. She couldn't look at the clock and say definitively it was 3:37 p.m. or whatever time it was. In all fairness, these days they don't spend a lot of time teaching how to read an analog clock in school. I jokingly told her I was *not* letting her go to college without having the ability to tell time on an analog clock, but I was totally serious. I felt like I was failing as a parent because she couldn't tell what time it was as soon as she looked at the clock. OK, I'm just kidding on this point, but I do think it is an important thing to know. So, here she is at seventeen years old, and I literally bought one of those clocks they use to teach grade school children to tell time and told her she needed to learn before she left for college. Lo and behold, she very quickly learned how to tell time on that clock. I finally felt like I was a success as a parent. In fact, I think I should get some sort of award or something. Just kidding! I digress. I do however still quiz her about it just to make sure she hasn't forgotten that important lesson. (She won't be too happy about me adding this to the book, but oh well.) I know many of you will be able to relate.

It seems silly to say, but these days many people can't tell time on an analog clock, especially Millennials and the newer generations that have followed them. As mentioned earlier, it is imperative to be able to tell time on an analog clock because it allows you to *see* the passage of time. That's why you should have at least one analog clock in your home. On an analog clock, you are actually watching the hands of the clock advancing. It shows movement, and it tells the brain that one minute is passing, then another and another. On a digital clock, your brain just sees a "number." While that number may represent the actual time at that moment, your brain is registering it in only one way. An analog clock represents the fact that time does not stand still, which is contrary to what is implied when looking at a digital clock. The number on a digital clock gives the illusion that time is still and stagnant.

Time is a funny thing. For the most part, time is something that most people take for granted. It's just one of those things that we don't really think about. It's like the Wi-Fi at your favorite coffee shop—always there, until it's not, and then you realize how much you needed it. We usually use it as a measure of when to be somewhere (like showing up fashionably late to that dinner party), how long we ought to do something (like convincing ourselves we'll work out for an hour, but actually just lying on the yoga mat), or when to get up in the morning (and how many times you hit the snooze button).

However you think about it (or not), time is always on the move. Whether you think about it or not, time is something that moves, it progresses. It's like a treadmill that never stops—except you're not burning any calories. Bummer, I know. It doesn't stay one "time" all day, which, as you might have guessed, is a natural misconception when you see the number on a digital clock.

The most important thing to know about time is this: once it passes, you can no longer get it back. It's like that last slice of cake—once it's gone, it's gone. You can't catch up on lost time, like trying to catch a bus that has already left the station. You can't buy time, even if you have a million dollars and a very persuasive argument. And borrowing against it? Not going to happen. Time is the ultimate nonrefundable, non-exchangeable, and definitely nonnegotiable resource.

The next time you glance at the clock, remember: time's ticking, and it's got places to be—just like you do. Don't let it slip through your fingers, because once it's gone, it's out there somewhere, probably having a great time without you.

"Lost time is never found again."

—BENJAMIN FRANKLIN

Here's a question for you: do you respect time? Sounds weird, right? How do you even respect something you can't see or hug? But have you ever really thought about if you actually respect time? You are probably asking yourself, what in the world is she talking about? But here's the thing—you have to have respect for something in order to appreciate and understand it. Just like you have respect for a person or a profession or an adorable puppy, it's necessary to have respect for a concept as well.

With that being said, the most important thing to know about time is that time is finite. That's right, I said it. News flash: time is finite! Meaning that once time passes, you can't get it back—period! Hard stop! This isn't anything new, but it is something that people don't often think about.

Cast your mind back to the days of yore when as a teen you may have slept until one or two in the afternoon. I know they say teens need more sleep, and we may all have done some of that, but we all can agree that sleeping the day away is pretty much a waste of "time." The reality is that you could be doing something else, anything else, productive or frivolous, but instead you chose to sleep away hours and hours of precious "time." Another visit to dreamland. You will never get those hours back. Why? Because they are gone, in the past, never to return again.

With the advent of communications technology, the same could be said when we spend countless hours scrolling the internet and our phones. It can suck so much time out of the day without our even realizing it. Guess what? You'll never get that time back. Once it's gone, it's gone! Sad but true. (OK, I think we've got that point now.)

What is important to understand here is that time is valuable. While you can't see it or hear it, it is an extremely important aspect of life. Once we gain respect for it, we learn to appreciate it and not waste it. Respecting time means acknowledging that every tick of the clock is a moment you could be using to make memories, achieve goals, or simply enjoy life. Time moves with or without you, so don't let it slip through your fingers like sand in an hourglass. Instead, treat it like the precious, nonrenewable resource it is, and make the most of every moment you have.

"Time waits for no one."

—UNKNOWN

Now that I've talked a little about time as a concept or theory, let's look at the correlation between clutter and time. We will look at how clutter affects your time mentally, physically, and visually, to name a few. All of these and more reflect the price you pay in terms of your time for having too much clutter. While you can't put a real monetary value on time, everything does have a price, in one way or another. After all, that is the purpose of this book.

There are many ways that your clutter robs you of your time. That may not make intuitive sense to you, but it is true. Let's look at the how and the why of it. According to the *Daily Mail*, a well-known news website, "Over the course of our lifetime, we will spend a total of 3,680 hours, or 153 days, searching for misplaced items." Holy cow! That sounds crazy, doesn't it? 153 days spent looking for stuff we actually have in our own homes? That equates to you losing almost half of a year over a lifetime. That's absurd! This statistic is pretty mind-blowing when you really think about it. In the words of Arsenio Hall, the late-night talk show host from the early '90s, it's one of those "things that make you say *hmmm*." (I'm dating myself, I know, but it is true.)

This has happened to all of us at some point. Even the most organized person will lose something and spend time looking for it. I myself have often organized things so well that I end up forgetting where I put something. Don't laugh at me, but it's true. Think about how many times this occurs in your own life; not the organizing part, but the looking for something part. Does it happen weekly, daily, or does it perhaps happen more than once a day? How often have you spent "time" looking for keys, phones, permission slips, glasses, and so on? I can almost guarantee it is more than once a day. When you live with clutter, this kind of scavenger hunt usually happens on a more regular basis than you'd like to admit. Your clutter is robbing you of minutes, hours, and maybe even weeks of valuable time that you can't get back—time that could have been spent doing something else, something more productive or enjoyable.

Imagine this: every time you're frantically searching for something, those minutes add up. Looking for things is obviously time-consuming. The truth of the matter is it doesn't have to be that way. Picture what you could accomplish if the time you spent looking for things was spent doing something that made you happy, that you actually enjoyed doing. Go ahead, dream. Dream big! Wouldn't it be more fun to spend that time with friends and family, on a hobby, attending a show, playing sports, or doing just about anything else? So, what do we do about it?

As was previously mentioned in the introduction, the ability to organize is a brain-based trait; essentially, your brain is either wired that way or it's not. It is something that comes naturally to you or it doesn't. If you are one of those people for whom organization doesn't come easily, you have to make an effort to keep the clutter under control and at bay. The clutter could be minimal or it could be taking over your entire home. Obviously, there are many reasons why this happens. I am not going to delve into great detail about the "why" in this book, but I will say that clutter can be situational, chronic, or even temporary. Whichever one you are dealing with, just know there is a light at the end of the tunnel.

* * *

Why does clutter happen? First and foremost, clutter occurs because there are no systems in place. What's a "system," you may ask? A system is simply orderliness or a method of doing something. The clutter mostly happens because we have too much stuff for the amount of space we live in. Systems are a way to keep the clutter at bay. Anything that we own needs to have a "home" in order for us to be able to live without clutter. If there is a place where each possession "lives," meaning a place where you will always find it, you will spend less time looking for that item. You and everyone else in the household will know exactly where to find it. There'll be no guessing, no asking someone where it is, and no searching and searching for said item.

You are probably wondering what it actually means for something to have a "home" or a place where it "lives." However you phrase it, quite simply, it means there is a place where you will find that item all the time, and most importantly, where it will be replaced after it is used.

There are many things that we give a "home" to unconsciously. For example, let's talk about brushing your teeth. You know exactly where to find your toothbrush and toothpaste because you put them in the same place every day as they have a place to "live." After all, I've never heard of anyone misplacing either item. This helps you and everyone else in the household locate it. (I'm talking about the toothpaste and not the toothbrush.) You use it, then you return it to its "home."

Someone else uses it, and then they return it to its "home;" easy-peasy. It's a very simple concept but not so easy to keep in practice. By retraining yourself to do this, over time it will become second nature for you and everyone else in the household. In the end, you will be managing the clutter and living more harmoniously.

Time plays a crucial role in this process. Initially, establishing these systems and habits may feel like a significant time investment. However, this upfront effort pays off by saving you countless hours in the future. Imagine the time you waste daily in searching for misplaced items; with a proper system, that time can be drastically reduced or even eliminated. Moreover, once these organizational habits become second nature, the time needed to maintain order diminishes as well. You will find that you spend less time tidying up and more time enjoying a clutter-free environment. Now, this doesn't mean that you won't have times where things get out of whack, systems get derailed, and some clutter might build up. But having the systems in place makes it a lot easier to get back on track. It might take some practice if this is not how your brain works naturally. You can either set the systems up yourself, or you can hire a professional organizer from one of the national associations (see the resource list in the back).

client story

Let me tell you about a client I once had. Meet Mary. (As with all client stories in this book, her name has been changed to protect her privacy.) Mary was a single mom with three wonderful kids between the ages of five and fifteen. The family was always living in chaos: toys and schoolwork were all over the house, laundry was piled to unbelievable levels, and they were always running late when they needed to go somewhere. The family was constantly buying multiples of the same item and rarely adhering to bedtime schedules because they were continually behind each day and trying to catch up on that day's activities. Does any of this sound familiar? While this may or not resonate with you, you may be wondering why this was their reality. Why was this their normal experience? The answer is simple...

unfortunate, but simple. Wait for it...you guessed it: they had no systems in place!

When I started working with this family, the first thing we did was to get their pile of dirty laundry clean. The fastest solution was to send it out to a laundry service. While there was obviously a cost for this, it was better to send it out than to spend hours doing it ourselves. Sometimes, your time is worth more than the dollars spent. (Side note: Mary liked this option so much that she decided to send her laundry out regularly.) Then we went room by room and sorted the items strewn all over into piles according to which room they really belonged in. Once the items were returned to their respective rooms, we went through everything in each room and purged what wasn't needed or wanted any longer. Finally, we organized what was left and gave everything a "home." Everything finally had a specific place where it would live. While this sounds quick and easy, please know that this did take time as there was quite a bit to get through.

Mary's problem was that, without a designated place for her belongings, she and her family were spending so much time searching for things that they didn't have time for the activities they enjoyed. No more clutter meant no more running late and no more delayed bedtimes.

"We function best in spaces that feel good. And usually, when they feel good, they look good."

—DEBBIE BOWIE

Remember the statistic mentioned earlier about the number of hours lost in a lifetime looking for things? It's 3,680 hours, to be exact. That's a staggering amount of time. The act of constantly looking for things not only wastes time but also leads to stress, which can snowball into a multitude of health issues. You don't need to be able to read tea leaves to know that's not a good outcome.

Let's try a little experiment. Take a moment to look at one of the piles or cluttered areas in your home. Let's face it, you know you have clutter or you wouldn't be reading this. No judgment, just fact. How do you feel when you look at that pile or area? Does it make you feel calm, tranquil, and peaceful, or does it give you anxiety, make you tense up, and leave you feeling irritable? I am guessing your answer is probably leaning more toward the latter. These are all signs of stress; whether you know it or not, your clutter is stressing you out.

You know you need to do something about it, but somehow it just hasn't happened. Maybe your idea of straightening up in a hurry is throwing things in bags and putting them in the closets when you are expecting company so no one else will see the clutter. While that may be an immediate solution, it is not solving the problem, not by a long shot. In fact, you are actually making matters worse. Hiding the clutter is a way to try to forget that you still have to deal with it. But then when you open the closets, *Bam!*—what you see is a vivid reminder that it has not gone away, and the stress creeps in again.

Just the mere fact that you are living with clutter means that you are probably looking for things on a regular basis. It really doesn't matter what it is you are looking for; you are usually looking for something. The angst and anxiety of rushing around in the scramble to find something is what is causing you stress. Believe it or not, the stress is manifesting in your body. You might not even realize that your headache or irritability or reactive outbursts are because of the stress caused by all the rushing and scrambling around looking for things. The culprit is the clutter in your home. It is a vicious cycle.

Not to mention that the more clutter you have, the more time will be spent on trying to maintain your home. All of the cleaning, vacuuming, and organizing will take far, far longer to get done—if you actually do it at all. Oftentimes there is so much clutter that it's just not possible to clean or vacuum properly. And even if you can clean or vacuum, it will take that much longer.

Time is so very precious and the clutter is stealing it from you. It keeps you stuck in a cycle of searching, stressing, and trying to catch up. The impact on your time and well-being is significant. Are you beginning to see that?

Let's just talk about the stress for a quick minute. Stress, time, and clutter are intricately related, forming a cycle that can significantly impact one's quality of life. Because of the clutter and the stress that it is causing, higher levels of stress can have an effect on your body and your mood, as well as your behavior. How exactly does it affect these areas, you may ask? I'll tell you.

Clutter consumes your time; wasted time increases your stress levels; stress affects your time management, and all of this impacts your quality of life. When your environment is cluttered, finding what you need becomes a time-consuming task. The extra time spent searching for items or cleaning up clutter leaves you feeling rushed and behind schedule. This constant state of urgency elevates stress levels, making you feel frazzled and overwhelmed. When you're stressed, your ability to manage time effectively decreases. This inefficiency leads to further time wasted and increases the stress related to time management. Stress and clutter reduce productivity. The more time you spend dealing with clutter, the less time you have for productive activities. This can hinder both personal and professional growth, affecting your overall quality of life. The reduction in leisure time can lead to burnout and a diminished sense of well-being.

According to research findings from the Mayo Clinic, muscle and/or chest pain, fatigue, upset stomach, change in sex drive, and sleep problems are just some of the potential effects of stress on your body, as well as headaches. In terms of the way it affects your mood, stress can cause anxiety, restlessness, lack of motivation, a feeling of being overwhelmed, depression, and of course irritability. Chronic effects of stress on your body and mind can include overeating or undereating, drug and/or alcohol abuse, tobacco use, social withdrawal, exercising less often, and angry outbursts. No one wants stress in their lives, but while it does happen, it can be avoided.

Imagine if you were able to remove the stress caused by your constant rushing and scrambling to find things and get it out of your life. Just think about how you would feel, not to mention the benefits to your body of having less stress—or even no stress. In addition, you would have more time in your day, week, and year. Oh my! What will you do? I, for one, can think of a million things I would love to do if I had more time to myself.

Recognizing and addressing the cycle of how clutter affects your time, in turn increasing your stress, is crucial for reclaiming your time, reducing stress, and improving your overall well-being. By breaking free from this cycle, you can create a more organized, efficient, and fulfilling life.

> *"Clutter is nothing more than postponed decisions."*
>
> —BARBARA HEMPHILL

client story

Let me introduce you to my client Susie. Susie was a single mom with one daughter. She was one of those people that was perpetually late. It didn't matter where she needed to go, she very rarely was on time. Her clutter made it nearly impossible for her to get anywhere in a timely fashion. To make a long story short, because of her issues with time and clutter, they quickly became the family's issues.

Her daughter's class was scheduled to go on a field trip. It was strongly impressed upon the parents that the bus would wait for no one, so they needed to be on time. The morning of the field trip, she couldn't find the permission slip. After searching and searching, Susie finally found it and they were on their way to the school. Unfortunately, it was too late. The bus had already left, which meant her daughter wasn't able to go on the field trip. Her daughter had quite the meltdown.

That was the straw that broke the camel's back. It was at that point that she knew she had to make a change, and she called a professional for help—a professional organizer, that is. Her disorganization was not only affecting her life but was now negatively impacting her daughter's life. It was time (no pun intended) for her to get help with the clutter and her time management.

"The best way to get something done is to begin."

—UNKNOWN

At one time or another, I am pretty sure that you have had some sort of gathering, party, or holiday event at your home. Of course, you have. You know the event is coming up, but you procrastinate getting your home in order, and before you know it, the week of the event is here, and then it's the day of the event. Panic sets in! You realize what needs to be done in preparation for the event. You have to go to the store for a couple of things, then there's the cooking and the decorating. Before you can even think about that, you remember the clutter. Oh no, first you have to deal with the clutter! What a time suck! When will you have the time with everything that needs to get done?

Part of you is scolding yourself, because if you had dealt with the clutter all along, you wouldn't be in this predicament now. Then you are wondering why you waited so long to deal with this since you had weeks to prepare. While your instinct may be to throw things in bags and boxes and toss them in the closet, that is not the best solution. That's just a temporary fix. That's basically just putting a band-aid over a cut that needs stitches. But why is this happening in the first place? The answer is because there are no systems and nothing you own has a home. This is yet another example of how the clutter is robbing you of your valuable, precious time. Remember, the more clutter, the more time-consuming it is to deal with the clutter.

"Clutter is not just physical stuff. It's old ideas, toxic relationships, and bad habits."

—ELEANOR BROWN

Are you a person who is good at making decisions, or are you indecisive? The clutter can have a tendency to cloud your mind, making it harder to focus and make decisions. If you are good at making decisions, that's great. However, if you are not decisive, that cloudiness could cost you a lot of time. I bet you are wondering how. Part of the process when managing clutter is doing a purge. As people in a modern society, we oftentimes acquire far more than we get rid of, which is in part what creates the clutter. So, when you are in the throes of the decluttering process and you are purging items, it is very helpful to be able to make firm decisions about what you want to do with an item. When you struggle with indecision, you may find it difficult to decide what to keep and what to let go of. While there are a variety of reasons for this indecisiveness, being indecisive certainly doesn't help in the process of managing clutter and organizing. It can lead to you keeping more than you need or have space for—which, of course, results in clutter.

Being indecisive can also affect your ability to allocate your time and resources to tackle the clutter. This can cause clutter to accumulate and become even worse as more items are acquired over time. In addition, indecisiveness can lead to a lack of clarity about what items are truly important or valuable to you and which of them aligns with your current needs and values. Without a clear sense of your priorities and preferences, it becomes challenging to declutter effectively. The bottom line is that all of this indecision is costing you precious time.

In addition, clutter can consume your time and energy as you navigate through a disorganized home, searching for items as a result of the clutter. The more time you spend managing the clutter or maneuvering around the clutter, the less time you have for other meaningful activities or pursuits.

As you can see there is a direct relationship between indecision, time, and clutter. It could be helpful to develop strategies for dealing with the indecision and/or to establish routines for regular decluttering and organization. Breaking down the process into manageable steps, making time for decluttering, and seeking the support of organizing professionals can all contribute to overcoming indecision and managing clutter effectively, thus giving you more time than you might currently have.

"For every minute spent organizing,
an hour is earned."

—UNKNOWN

One of the most important things that I hope you are getting from this chapter is that your time is precious and valuable. Respect it and honor it. Yet, there is another way to look at clutter, which takes the form of time clutter. Time clutter, as I like to call it (a Robynism), can show up in many forms. That may be a foreign term for you, but let me explain. Are you the go-to person that is always the one everyone asks when they need a favor? Are you one of those folks that gives of themselves for others on a continuous basis? Are you always saying yes to someone else, while putting your needs aside? What I am talking about is when someone else is infringing on your time by asking things of you. Ponder this for a while. Take a moment and think about your own situation. It may be taking someone else's kids home from a soccer game before doing the family shopping or helping to watch a friend's children, knowing you will have to cancel your hair appointment, or doing just about anything that someone else is asking of you despite what may be more pressing in your own life. Now, I'm not an ogre. I understand that we should all help one another on occasion because we all need help as well, but the question is, how often should we put others first, and at what expense?

If this resonated with you or if you are constantly saying yes when asked to help others, you are more concerned with someone else's needs at the expense of your own. Of course, you don't want to be taken advantage of, but that can quite easily happen. People that are in the habit of doing this have a need to make others happy, which usually comes at a cost to their own time, mental health, money, etc.—the essential part being your time. For our purposes, why people often do this is not as important as the mere fact that they do it at all. Since time is something that cannot be exchanged, recouped, or caught up on, by giving in to someone else's needs, you are giving away a very valuable resource. Please remember that your time is just as precious and valuable to you as your time is to someone else. Just offering you another way to think of how time clutter is affecting you.

* * *

The key is consistency and patience, knowing that every minute spent organizing is an investment in a more efficient and stress-free future, an investment that can save you time in a variety of ways. The mental clarity and reduced stress that comes from a clutter-free environment can lead to more productive and focused use of your time in all areas of your life. By embracing organization, you are reclaiming your time and enhancing your overall well-being.

space

"Picture your dream home.
I bet it's not filled with clutter."

—JOSHUA BECKER,

The Minimalist Home: A Room-by-Room Guide to a Decluttered, Refocused Life

When you hear the word "space," what comes to mind? Perhaps it's something in outer space like the moon; maybe it's your personal space, the area around your person; it could be your physical space, as in where you live; or the space in your brain, otherwise known as mental space. Well, as a certified professional organizer, when I think of "space," I think of both our physical space, which is where we live, and our mental space, what is in our brains. With that said, let's dive in and examine how the concept of "space" relates to our clutter, both physical and mental.

It has been said that the average home contains 300,000 items (as reported in an *LA Times* article). I was actually in utter disbelief myself when I first heard this. I know it may sound completely ridiculous, but when you think of everything that you own—every utensil, sock, tool, bathroom product, dish, toy, and so on—it is most certainly true. I even considered counting all the items in my home, but then I thought that might not be the best use of my time. But I digress; let's get back on topic.

What adds to the amount of things in your home is if you get items for free. Somehow that gives us license to take way more than we would ever need. We are all guilty of this...trust me. I know I have been guilty of doing this myself on more than one occasion. Then I realized that not only did I not need the free item, but I certainly didn't need several. Years ago, I remember working with a client that had so many sample-size toiletries—you know, the ones you get from hotels when you travel—that I am convinced he would pour the entire maid's cart of samples into his suitcase. I'm only kidding, but that's what it seemed like, because there were so many in his home. They literally had bags and bags and bags of samples. After a bit of convincing, the client realized they didn't need all of them. The client willingly let most of them go and donated them to a homeless shelter.

I'm going to let you in on a little secret. Believe it or not, the amount of space we live in is finite. There's that word again. Shocking, I know! But think about it, it's true; the size of the space is the size of the space. That is pure fact. As much as we wish we could, unlike Harry Potter, we do not have the ability to wave a magic wand and make the closets bigger or the rooms in our home more spacious. Sadly, we just don't possess that kind of power, no matter how much we would like to have such abilities. So that means we have to live within the confines of our four walls. What we own, and more importantly, what we choose to keep in our homes is completely within our control. Let me say it again for the people in the back: what we allow into our space is completely dictated by our own choices. The number of things we own is because we have made a decision to bring them all into our homes. So, if we choose to live in clutter, that is a choice we make, whether it is a conscious or unconscious choice. While having all of that "stuff" might not be the best choice, it is nonetheless a choice. So how much stuff is too much?

Don't get me wrong. I completely understand that there are certain situations and health circumstances that may make the choice of whether to bring stuff into the home more challenging. Mental health issues can play a big part in this, but I am speaking more from a general standpoint that includes someone who doesn't have those kinds of issues. For a variety of reasons, it may be a challenge to limit the number of things in your home and to keep your home and other spaces organized, but all of us have a choice in how we live. As with other things, if you are not good at something, then you can always hire a professional to do it for you or assist you with it, if it is within your means. It's true what they say: our home is our sanctuary and our happy place—or at least it should be. After all, with so much going on in our lives both mentally and physically, our home should be a place where we can relax, release, and reset.

We all know that unexpected things can happen at any time. There are floods, fires, earthquakes, tornadoes, and much more. However, we never think it is going to happen to us or where we live. But what if it did? What if there was an emergency and you needed to leave your home right away? Imagine for a minute that the exits were obstructed and you couldn't get out because of the clutter. What would happen then? Or maybe you might need access to safety equipment, and you couldn't get to it because of the clutter? It may sound somewhat extreme, but I have had clients where the clutter is so bad that these things were blocked and not easily accessible. This doesn't sound like a recipe for success; quite the contrary.

Now let's get to the root of things. How does clutter relate to the "physical space" in your home? What is the clutter costing you in terms of physical space? My sense is that the goal should always be to feel comfortable in your home, to be able to move freely within the space and for your home to be a place where you can refresh and rejuvenate yourself. It should be more than just a place to come in out of the rain or somewhere to lay your head at night. In order for this to be true, you should only keep what fits comfortably within the home, which includes the closets and the cabinets as well as perhaps even a garage or outdoor shed or similar on-site storage resources. The goal is to not have things hanging from furniture, living on floors, or spilling out of the closets or cabinets when you open the doors. One of the reasons this happens is because there is too much stuff. Another reason is because things aren't put back into their "home," they get shoved wherever they can fit when it comes time to tidy up. In addition, what often happens is that when something can't fit in its designated space, it will be put someplace else where you wouldn't think of finding it again. Does that resonate with you at all? Does it sound familiar? Does it hit a nerve?

While it's not meant to be triggering, it is meant to get you to think about your own home and how you could live differently and do better. Although it may sound pretty simple, it's not always as easy in practice. That's because people living with clutter usually have far more than they need and often don't realize it. They sometimes feel that they need everything they have. If they do realize that their possessions exceed their space, they often don't take the time to do anything about it. Their belongings are often shoved—and I mean *shoved*—into closets and drawers and cabinets in order to "hide it" so that the clutter is not all over the place. This method is what many people mean when they say they are tidying up; in many cases, when they are expecting someone over to the house. This obviously is not the most practical way to deal with your clutter. So let me ask you this. What good is having all that stuff if you are not using it all or honoring it? By that I mean taking care of it in the proper way. Shoving your belongings in closets as a place for them to live is by far not the best solution. But it is very common for people to do this.

Many times, when I am working with clients and we are organizing the kitchen or bedrooms, or any area with drawers, it is sometimes a challenge to open the drawers because they are so full of stuff that they get stuck. It can be so frustrating for the person living there that they will ignore the fact that the drawer is overstuffed, and they might not even bother trying to fix the issue. By "fix the issue," I mean clear out the drawers. Instead, they simply use the drawers they can open, or they'll force another open and shove the things inside in order to close them away. When they can't find what might be in said drawers, they will sometimes just buy another one. When things get really bad and they run out of storage space, they move on to Plan B: using some sort of bin or perhaps getting another bureau or cabinet.

Don't start beating yourself up about this, because you are certainly not the only person dealing with things in this way. I see it all the time when I am working with clients. There are so many questions that come to mind for me: Why is this the solution? Why do you think you do this? Why is it happening at all? Why do people keep more than they need? What is it about human nature that causes them to hold onto things whether they need them or not? We all know our space is only so big. We know that we only have space for so much, and yet we continue to bring more and more into the home. But why? That is such a loaded can of worms since there are many reasons for this behavior.

Stuff that comes into the home gets there by a variety of means. Many people love to shop and use the activity as retail therapy (or addiction), relief from boredom, and as a time for socializing, to name just a few reasons. So often, the act of shopping and buying soothes the soul when someone is feeling down. People can sometimes have a shopping addiction; these days, that shopping pursuit usually happens more online, but the result is the same...more objects coming into the home. We get bored and we shop because it gets us out of the house and doing something. Or we get together with friends and go shopping as a way to socialize together. I have also noticed that people love free stuff, and it doesn't matter if they need it or not. Just the mere fact that it is free gives people the permission to take more than one. This adds unnecessarily to the clutter. They may not need the item or even like it but will take it anyway, perhaps thinking they will give it to someone else or find some sort of use for it.

Then there are those people who buy very expensive things and don't want to let something go because they spent so much money on the item. That extra stuff will accumulate over time, adding to the clutter. Then there are those who have sentimental attachments to items, rational or not. This could be a whole chapter by itself. Let's not forget about the grandparents who keep buying toys for the grandkids whenever they see them. It's as if they feel the need to reward the grandkids with a toy just for being alive. These are just some of the ways stuff keeps coming into our homes, but there are countless others. One thing I always say to my clients is, "We are an abundant society, and we bring much more into our homes than we take out." Personally, I blame it on the advent of credit cards. This misguided concept makes people feel that they can afford anything they want when they want it. But I digress. More on that in another chapter.

> *"1 out of every 10 Americans rent off-site storage—the fastest growing segment of the commercial real estate industry over the past four decades."*
>
> **—JOSHUA BECKER,**
>
> "21 Surprising Statistics That Reveal How Much Stuff We Actually Own", Becoming Minimalist

Speaking of abundance and space, when the space tends to fill up in the home, people may often opt for off-site storage. According to Self-Storage Almanac, there are over 51,000 storage facilities in the United States. It's true that off-site storage can serve a useful purpose. Perhaps you are doing a home remodel and you need to store your furniture while the work is being done, or maybe you are between homes because you have to move out of your old home before you can move into the new home. On occasion, a client who travels a tremendous amount for work will give up their rental or rent out their home because they will be gone for extended periods of time, and they may choose to put their personal belongings in storage. These are examples of when off-site storage could be useful.

However, if you are putting things in storage because you have run out of room in your home, that would be a big no-no. When people run out of space in their home, they often want to put their "extra" stuff in storage. But most good professional organizers will tell you that off-site storage should be a temporary solution, not a long-term solution. While the intention might be to store the items for only weeks or perhaps a few months, before you know it, years have gone by. When that much time has passed, it is quite possible that you no longer even know what is in the storage unit(s). This is when storage becomes a black hole.

client story

Meet Joan. Joan is a lovely older woman with two grown sons. When we started working together, I was initially helping her declutter her condo, the contents of which included various collections. You could tell that she definitely liked to shop. She had a large collection of purses, among other things. During our discussions, it was revealed that she had not one, but *two* storage units, and she'd had them for over ten years. Because she never went to the units, she didn't even remember what was in them. (This is a common theme for people.) Remember when I mentioned how storage units become a black hole? This is exactly what I mean. When the client and I calculated the amount of money she'd spent on those two storage units over that ten years, it was well over $20,000. That is a significant amount of money. Imagine what she could have spent that money on instead. The unfortunate part is that she couldn't even remember what she was storing. That likely means it wasn't that meaningful or necessary to begin with.

In today's world, life outside the home can be very chaotic. We work long hours; we are running around from here to there trying to take care of all of our commitments. That's why when we finally get home after a long day of hustle and bustle, our home should be a sanctuary, a place of peace to get away from the turmoil of the outside world. It may sound like a cliché, but how many people enjoy coming home to their four walls that are riddled with chaos? If you actually polled a variety of people and asked them to describe the feeling of their ideal home, I am pretty sure that most people would say they want their home to be clean, calm, comfortable, organized, and peaceful. How many people do you think live in a home that fits these descriptors? If you actually saw where most of those people were living, it's doubtful that the words above would be an accurate way to describe their current living situation.

You know I love a statistic, so here's another one for you. The National Association of Home Builders reports that the average home size was 983 square feet in 1950, 1,500 square feet in 1970, and 2,349 square feet in 2004. The median size of a newly built home in 2021 was 2,532 square feet. In today's housing market, the current trend is to build what are being called "McMansions." These cover almost the entire lot, leaving very little yard space. The fact that these homes and others are twice as large or even larger than they were in the last century is part of the problem. The bigger the space, the more stuff we will own. Just like the more money you make, the more money you spend...generally. Sometimes the size of the home doesn't really even matter because many will often opt for off-site storage just to store many of their belongings that won't fit in their home or that they cannot part with, as we have already mentioned.

Another reason that we may be overrun by clutter has to do with the closet space in our homes. Older homes had very few closets, and the ones they had tended to be quite small, indicating that people didn't own as many things. Years ago, if you didn't have the cash, you couldn't buy something—more on that later. Now walk-in closets have become the norm. Where they were once considered a luxury in a home, they are now to be expected for those looking to buy. Folks will literally salivate over a spacious walk-in closet when they are touring homes. They are a huge selling feature and the return on investment for the builder is close to 100 percent. Not bad, but I digress. These larger types of closets allow us to store all the stuff we accumulate—or at least that's the goal.

We previously talked about the fact that having less time can add to one's stress level, which can possibly lead to health issues. But living with clutter in a limited amount of space can also lead to health issues over time, as well as it being a safety hazard and even downright dangerous. Is this anything you had ever thought about? I would bet that most people have never considered this. We all know that clutter doesn't just live in cabinets and closets. It is often on every surface, every tabletop, every chair, and every space that is available. Of course, that means it can also live on the floor. Trust when I say I am pretty sure that it is not living there in an orderly fashion. Many times, there won't just be clothes all over the floor, but also toys, pens, bags, dishes, and books; you name it and it could find its way to a life on the floor. This makes it much more challenging as well as possibly even dangerous to walk around our own homes. We have to step over things, kick things out of the way, or even pile things on top of one another just to get around. Imagine what would happen if you were rushing around and not paying attention. It would be very easy to trip and fall because of all the stuff on the floor. Imagine what could happen if you had mobility issues and needed a cane or crutches or perhaps braces to move around. How would the clutter on the floor affect you then? It becomes a major issue for people with mobility challenges, whether or not they created the clutter or are just living with it.

When we live alone, we basically have no one to think about but ourselves, so the clutter being a hazard to the safety of others may not be top-of-mind. What we do and how we do it doesn't necessarily impact anyone else—unless of course you invite people into your home. Many times, that doesn't happen because of the state of someone's home. However, when we live with other people, it would be considerate to take into account the fact that the conditions of the home are affecting them as well. Whether it is our children, our parents, or anyone with mobility issues, the amount of stuff in the home can be a hazard to them as well as to us. Even if someone who lives in the home is our polar opposite and doesn't like the clutter, we should try and remember that it is not all about us. Once again, what we do and the way we do it does indeed affect other people.

"Clutter is not just the stuff on your floor—it's anything that stands between you and the life you want to be living."

—PETER WALSH

Over the years, I have had numerous clients who have become rather antisocial because they don't want other people coming into their homes. It can even take them a long time to get up the courage to hire a professional organizer such as myself to come into their home so they can get help with their clutter. They are usually very embarrassed to let others see how they are living. They just need to remember that we come with no judgment, we are just there to help. The question they often ask me is how they stack up against other clients I have had. Clients always think their own situation is the worst. Very rarely are they the worst I have seen. When you have been doing this work for as long as I have, nothing can truly surprise you anymore. I have a little thing I say to my clients to lighten the situation and put them at ease: I tell them they need to think of me as their doctor. If they had a rash on their butt, they would go to the appointment, drop their britches, and show the doctor the rash. No judgment, no embarrassment; you just go because you need to get some relief for your rash. There's no difference when working with a professional organizer. Our goal is strictly to give you the help you need. We are completely nonjudgmental. Go and get that rash taken care of!

It is quite normal for a client to be full of anxiety at the idea of guests coming over. Clients can be frozen with fear at the thought of allowing others to witness how they live, so much so that they don't ever have people over. They often retreat into themselves to avoid the embarrassment and may no longer socialize the way they want to. I have seen this time and time again: clients who were once outgoing and very social have become homebodies and hermits. Your clutter should never have such a hold on you that it changes who you are and what you do. Even though their cluttered home isn't literally following them around, it weighs on their minds, and they often feel as if everyone knows. Of course, this isn't true, but it frequently affects how they live their lives. Their cluttered space is causing them to live inauthentically—to live as someone they are not. It is very sad to see how a plethora of stuff can change who someone is in a functional sense and how they live their life.

"Control your clutter or it will control you."

—ALEJANDRA COSTELLO

Another way your space is impacted by clutter is by the things we all accumulate that we love so dearly. One of the things I have realized over my many years of working with clients, in addition to the numerous home cleanouts I have done, is that everyone has their own personal museum of something. It is always interesting to see what that something actually is. I have seen collections of items as small as thimbles and perfume bottles, and I have seen collections of things as big as Lego sets that are completely constructed. Imagine finding space in your home for the Lego Taj Mahal or the Lego Eiffel Tower, or even a roller coaster. I have even had a client who liked to collect Birkin bags. They were on a shelf at the top of the closet that went around the whole space, almost like a train set in a store. And no, I'm not kidding! It may not have been a collection to her, but I certainly considered it a collection due to the sheer number of bags she owned.

Then there are those who like certain animals; they may have chicken pot holders, chicken napkin rings, framed chicken art, statues of chickens, and so on. Trust me when I say I have seen it all! Please know that I am not talking about a few collectibles that may take up a shelf or two. I'm talking about collections on such a large scale that they seem to take over your home, whether intentionally or not; the kind that is noticeable as soon as you enter the home or the room where it is kept. The reason I bring this up is because excessive collections like these can often become clutter as well. Once the collections overflow from the shelves to the floor, that is when it becomes clutter. Collections become displaced. It becomes clutter when the floor is the only place left to display the items. I want you to keep in mind that there is a distinct difference between collecting a few things you like and having so many that the collection is taking over your home and is now becoming clutter. So, tell me...what are you collecting?

The organizing industry has become so popular these days that there are many TV shows that depict different aspects of the industry. Most of the shows are about home design and organizing, but there are also those that show the extremes of clutter such as *Hoarders* and *Hoarding: Buried Alive*. These shows have become extremely popular. Talk about clutter affecting our space. These shows exhibit the worst examples of clutter. In fact, in 2013, hoarding disorder officially became diagnosable as a mental illness listed in the *DSM-5* diagnostic handbook. Human nature being what it is, people just love a "train wreck." The same way we like to stop and watch any kind of accident, people become mesmerized by what they see on these shows. Why is it we get fixated on something and it becomes an obsession? Why is it that when we see something so disturbing, we somehow can't not watch? The fact that we as humans are often compelled by the sight of what strikes us as extreme and outlandish has become a profitable incentive for TV shows based on such material, and successful ones at that. *Extreme Collectors* was another one of those shows; there have been others related to over-the-top collections, but although it was short-lived, this one was very popular. The point here is it's a long way from collecting a few things that fit in a cabinet or on a shelf to going to the extreme, where it takes over the room or even the house. This is without a doubt a much bigger problem.

"The more things you own,
the more they own you."

—UNKNOWN

There are many life changes that can force you to declutter your space in order to create more room; for instance, if you get married or otherwise move in with someone and combine two households, or if someone leaves you all of their stuff when they pass away, or even if you are simply moving to a new residence. These are all scenarios where it makes sense to purge what you have. After all, the 80/20 rule is alive and well. In case you don't know what that is, the 80/20 rule says we use 20 percent of what we own 80 percent of the time. (The 80/20 rule, also known as the Pareto Principle, was discovered by Vilfredo Pareto.) Think about this in terms of your own wardrobe. We all have a closet (or more than one) full of clothes. Yet, when we get dressed, we end up going to those same twenty or so pieces of clothing. We all do it, even me. Those are our favorites that we like, that fit well, that we feel comfortable in, and that look good on us. Am I right? I'm guessing I probably am.

client story

Meet Lisa. Lisa was at a point in her life where she wanted to get her closet more organized. It was so full that she couldn't even see what she owned. There were clothes everywhere. They were thrown (and I do mean thrown) on the shelves, and they were scattered all over the floor and on top of every surface. We went through every item in the closet one by one, and in the end, she let go of several bags of clothes that no longer served her. If I remember correctly, it was four large trash bags full. Most of it was stuff she hadn't even seen or worn in years. When we finished, she was absolutely delighted. Not only could she now see what she owned, but it was easier for her to get dressed because she wasn't struggling to see her clothes and she had easier access to each garment. Since we couldn't make the walls of the closet any bigger, she reevaluated what was important to her to meet the confines of the space.

"Make space in your life for what matters."

—UNKNOWN

While decluttering or purging is a great way to get an understanding of what you own, it will also make it easier to store those items. However, there is another solution as well. This is in no way meant to be an excuse for you to keep everything but rather a solution to help get things more organized. The answer is to redesign your closets and space. Designing a custom closet for your space will allow you to truly maximize your space and utilize it more effectively. This could be a system designed for your exact needs inside a closet or it could be a wall unit in a room. Regardless of where it is, a customized system is bound to create more space and allow you to better store and organize what you own. It doesn't have to break the bank either. There are so many options available that you can purchase from a store, or you can have a custom closet built by a variety of closet companies or cabinet makers. Trust me when I say a custom closet will create space where there seemingly isn't any. In my opinion, it's everyone's dream. Or at least it should be. Moving on.

I can only imagine that your head is probably spinning with all this information as this has probably already been a lot to wrap your head around. But there's more! Now that we've covered how clutter relates to our physical space, let's talk about the relationship of clutter to *mental* space, meaning the space in our brains—a.k.a. mental clutter. Physical clutter can have a significant impact on our mental well-being and mental space. Let's examine the different ways this happens.

Before we move on, I'd like you to try an experiment. Go to an area of your home and look at the clutter. If you don't have any clutter, then look at a picture of a cluttered home. What comes to mind when you see it? What's your first reaction? How does it make you feel? I would pretty much bet that it doesn't make you feel all warm and fuzzy—quite the contrary, I would imagine. Seeing the clutter probably stresses you out and makes you feel uneasy, anxious, and dare I say, overwhelmed. That is quite common. Clutter can often make it difficult to focus, which in effect makes you less productive and makes decision making much harder. After all, the dictionary definition of the verb "clutter," according to Merriam-Webster, is "to fill or cover with scattered or disordered things that impede movement or reduce effectiveness." The way that the clutter crowds your physical space affects how your brain feels when it sees the clutter. Your brain is probably spiraling in all different directions—at least, mine is. I imagine a tornado in my head at the sight of clutter and not being able to stop its spiral. Obviously, that isn't the reality, but just thinking about it as I write this is making my brain spin. Auntie Em, Auntie Em! Hold on, Toto! I digress. The point I am trying to make is that the physical clutter creates mental clutter and can make you mentally stagnant, less productive, and unfocused, which again can lead to stress. And we all know by now that stress is not good for our overall health.

client story

Allow me to introduce you to Cynthia. Cynthia is chronically disorganized. (The definition of chronic disorganization is "having a past history of disorganization in which self-help efforts to change have failed, [and there is] an undermining of current quality of life due to disorganization and the expectation of future disorganization," according to the Institute for Challenging Disorganization; learn more at www.icd.org.)

She had a habit that when she took something out, it never really found itself back to where it belonged. It was as if she needed to see it to know that she owned it. It didn't really matter what the item was. Needless to say, there were things everywhere. The kitchen counters were packed with everything you could imagine, and the dining table was overrun with stuff, as well as every chair, floor, and surface. Wherever it could fit, it did. The clutter in her home made it very hard for her to focus on things she needed to accomplish, even basic everyday tasks like cleaning, repairs, food shopping, and so forth.

Once we were able to get her clutter under control and implement systems for her to do things differently, it completely changed her life.

"Clutter is the physical manifestation of stress."

—DEBBIE BOWIE

As previously mentioned, excessive physical clutter creates a certain amount of stress that you live with daily. When physical clutter is crowding your physical space, it's hard to forget that it's there, which makes it very hard to relax. How are you supposed to rest and reset when you are living in chaos? The same is true for your mental clutter. This is a very important point that we have yet to discuss. The mental clutter, or the spiraling of your brain, as I call it, can affect you just as much as the physical clutter; in some cases, it can affect you even more. It has great potential to reduce your productivity, which can easily make you stagnant. People usually equate productivity with their job or their home office, but mental clutter can affect more than just your work. It can also have a great effect on *residential productivity*. This is a term you may not be familiar with, meaning anything that is related to the care of your home. This includes things like taking care of home repairs, cleaning, laundry, food shopping, and much more, including coordinating activities and making doctor appointments. When we become stagnant for any reason, it can often have an impact on many areas of our lives. I have even seen instances where it affects one's desire for personal hygiene and eating. This is obviously a much bigger problem.

Let's delve into this a little further. As you read this, I really want you to be honest with yourself and see if any of these things resonate with you in thinking about mental clutter and your level of residential productivity.

- When you get overwhelmed by mental clutter, do you find you become unmotivated?
- When you get overwhelmed by mental clutter, do you feel like cleaning the house?

- When you get overwhelmed by mental clutter, are you motivated to do the laundry?
- When you get overwhelmed by mental clutter, are you interested in food shopping and cooking?
- When you get overwhelmed by mental clutter, is paying your bills high on your priority list?

If any of these questions resonate with you (and I could have asked you to consider a million more), then the mental clutter is taking control and making you less productive. Please know that it is not a conscious choice but just something that happens. Believe me when I say that you are not alone. You are one of many who struggle with this same reality.

There is also an emotional impact that comes along with the mental clutter. As your brain is swirling, twirling, or doing cartwheels, and you are telling yourself you should be doing X, Y, and Z, one can often feel guilt, shame, frustration, and a lack of control. That's because you know you should be doing something and be productive in some way, but you aren't motivated so you end up doing nothing at all. This demonstrates how the mental clutter is just as much of a barrier as the physical clutter.

"Happiness is a place between too little and too much."

—FINNISH PROVERB

Did you know there is a correlation between mental clutter and creativity as well? The mental clutter can be so powerful that it can smother your creativity. If you are a creative person, you may have noticed that your creativity is limited when your brain is cluttered. It is much harder to develop new ideas and think creatively when the physical clutter in your space generates mental clutter in your brain. Take a pause and think about this for a minute. Are you able to be and do your best when your mind is cluttered? Or do you feel stagnant and stuck, unable to create? Does this ring true for you? I am guessing it just might.

When a space is nicely organized and has a feeling of calm and order, it encourages creativity and productivity. I know that to be true for myself, as

I found out even before beginning my career as a professional organizer. At various times in my life, things have felt a little off in my home; there was a somewhat off-putting feeling, I would say—so much so that my creativity and productivity were completely stifled. It wasn't until I created an environment that was peaceful and harmonious that my home once more became a place that was conducive to my being creative and productive. What do you need in your home to make you feel creative and able to accomplish what you set out to do? Maybe it's just a candle burning, or having fresh flowers in your home, or music playing, or maybe it's your space being free of clutter. Whatever it is, it makes a difference.

There's one more thing I would like to mention when we talk about the relationship between space and clutter. Recently there have been many TV shows that have brought hoarding into the public's awareness. As previously mentioned, it is actually a diagnosable mental illness that involves a person living in a home that is overrun by an extreme quantity of stuff, often piled as high as the ceiling, where things are taking over every room in the home. You can probably visualize what that looks like, or perhaps you have seen one of the TV shows about hoarding. Obviously, if someone is living in these conditions, it is dangerous for them to navigate the space and to do everyday tasks like cooking, bathing, cleaning, and so on. Even though this is an important correlation between the level of clutter and usefulness of the space, it is not the thing I want to explore. The point I want to make is that if you are living with most of your home overrun with stuff, and I mean really overrun, as in there is so much clutter it constitutes a hoard, you are not living alone. It is a guarantee that there are critters living in the home as well. So not only is the clutter taking over your home, but it is attracting roaches, mice, and/or rats as well. That will also mean that there will be a stench in the home from the defecation of these rodents. None of this is healthy or sanitary for you, or for anyone or anything else (as in pets) living in your home. This is the extreme, but it is very important to mention because sometimes people don't realize the way they are living.

While it may be a cliché, your home is your sanctuary and should always be a place to relax and reset. An abundance of clutter makes it hard to do that.

money

"Collect moments, not things."

—UNKNOWN

In this chapter, we are going to explore the relationship between clutter and money. Some connections will be obvious, while others may be new to you. There is so much that can be said about money, and there are so many idioms about money: "money is the root of all evil," "money doesn't grow on trees," "money doesn't buy happiness," and *so* many more. I would imagine that you grew up hearing a lot of these idioms from your parents. They were definitely abundant in my house. I started looking into the origin of some of these, but there were too many and their origins were way too involved to mention here. Let's get back to the relationship between money and clutter. As previously mentioned, the average home contains about 300,000 items. I don't know about you, but it's hard to imagine having that many items in my home. It's even harder to imagine what that equates to when you convert it into dollars.

Another Robynism that I always say to my clients is, "We live in an abundant society, and we get much more than we get rid of." I'd like you to take a look around in your own home and just imagine how much money has been spent on all of the things in it. So much can be said about why we, as consumers, obtain so many things. Let's face it—we are definitely a consumer-driven society. Everywhere you look, we are conditioned into believing that you need this thing or that thing. The messaging is all around us. In fact, it's hard to avoid it. However, discussing the real reasons goes much, much deeper. That itself could be a whole chapter and I would imagine there are countless books on the subject.

For the purposes of this book, let's talk about a few things. Why is it that we have so much stuff these days? If you look at old houses that were built in the 1920s to

1940s, homes had very small closets and small kitchens. That's because people didn't own as many things. Life was a lot simpler, and we didn't feel the need to acquire as much. This we already know. As far as a "why" is concerned, I believe it is partly because of the advent of credit cards. Even though the first credit cards were used in the early 1950s, they didn't gain popularity until the 1960s. Credit cards gave us more purchasing power, they gave us the ability to buy higher priced items, and using them also gave license to impulse buying, which has led us to becoming a consumer culture of materialism. I believe that impulse buying is a huge part of why we live with clutter. There are many reasons why people make impulse purchases: depression, boredom, and filling a void (even though this may not be a conscious decision) are a few that are top-of-mind. But then there's also the fact that shopping can be a social activity. You decide that you and your friends want to hang out, so you go to the mall. You know that you shouldn't be buying anything because it's not in your budget right now. You know you shouldn't spend any money on anything. You know you don't need anything, plus you have other things to put that money toward. Then it happens: you see that amazing handbag or that fabulous pair of shoes, and you simply must have it! You try to remind yourself that you weren't going to buy anything, but then you realize there is a credit card burning a hole in your pocket. Credit cards give you false permission to buy that item. Instant gratification! You don't have to worry about paying for it now, you will deal with that later when the bill comes. At the moment when you are making the purchase, it's not even part of your thought process that it actually costs money, you just want that item. Credit cards = instant gratification = clutter.

There are many times when credit cards can be a real blessing, especially if there is an emergency. I'm talking about a true emergency, like needing to immediately fly home because your mother is dying (this actually happened to me) or having to get a new tire because one of your car's tires has a nail in it and you have no spare. What is *not* an emergency is feeling like the world will come to an end if you don't buy those red bottom shoes today since it's the last pair in your size. Credit cards tell us we can afford something in the moment that we shouldn't be buying at all. It gives us a misconstrued sense of affordability. Sometimes we are willing to pay more for an item than we would normally be willing to spend if we were paying cash. We get into the habit of using them repeatedly and often end up with lots of debt, and then we stress about how we are going to pay it back. The point is that because credit cards allow us to buy things whenever we want, we often clutter up our homes with mostly unnecessary things. We are bringing more and more items into our homes, whether we need them or not, which adds to the clutter. More times than not, when we bring things in, we are not getting rid of anything in exchange, so the clutter builds up more and more. Instead of only getting things we need—and I mean truly *need*—we are acquiring things that we want instead.

Speaking of wants and needs, let's talk for a minute about what the difference is between the two. According to Dictionary.com, a need is a requirement, while a want is something that is desired. Food is a need since human beings must have food in order to give our bodies the sustenance to live. However, that eighth pair of black shoes? That is a want, especially since you already have seven other pairs. We need a place to live for shelter and security, but we want to go on a vacation for enjoyment and relaxation. See where I'm going with this? Needs are essential, wants are extra. Needs are the fundamental things we can't live without, while wants are the nice-to-haves that make life more enjoyable but aren't necessary for survival.

Now, here's the kicker: your wants are draining your money. When you spend on wants, you often buy things with no real value or lasting significance. This money could be better spent on necessities or saved for important goals like retirement, emergencies, or investments. According to Yahoo.com, one in four Americans has no retirement savings. That's a staggering statistic, one that should be a wake-up call. It's crucial to prioritize our financial well-being over our fleeting desires.

With so many "wants," so often, the object we wanted doesn't get used and sits in a drawer or closet collecting dust (metaphorically speaking). Think about that gadget you bought on a whim, or those trendy clothes that never see the light of day. These items represent wasted money and missed opportunities to allocate resources more wisely. It's easy to get caught up in the excitement of acquiring something new, but it's important to ask ourselves: Does this add value to my life? Is it worth the financial trade-off?

When people spend money on impulse buys or other unnecessary items, especially when they know they can't afford to buy the item, don't have the space, or really don't need it, it starts to stress them out. The inward conversation can sound something like "how will I pay the bill," "why" did I buy that," "I could have used that money on x, or y, or z." It can eventually become buyer's remorse. All of this angst can lead to a cluttered mind, and as we discussed previously, stress can lead to a whole other set of problems. So why buy that unneeded item when you will probably be stressed out in the end? Before making an unnecessary expenditure, you should ask yourself if it is really worth it.

Understanding the distinction between wants and needs and learning to manage our desires is crucial for financial stability and peace of mind. It's about making conscious choices that align with our long-term goals and recognizing that while wants can bring temporary joy, they often don't contribute to lasting fulfillment. By prioritizing needs and being mindful of our spending, we can build a more secure financial future and make room for truly meaningful experiences and investments in our lives.

client story

When I think of how your clutter affects your money, I think of a lovely client I had years ago named Pat. She was a single older woman who had been living in her house for nearly thirty years. Her home was a good-sized, two-story, 2,200-square-foot house with three bedrooms where she lived alone. Unfortunately, she had a shopping problem; her home was filled with clothes, toys, toiletries, and much more. She was living with clutter in every room, although she may not have thought so. All of the closets in each bedroom were packed with clothes. In addition, each bedroom had two rolling racks of clothes and clothing strewn across every surface, including on the bed, the top of the dresser, and chairs, plus the floor was piled with bags of more stuff. It didn't end there. There was also a two-car garage full of stuff, a small pool cabana full of stuff, and a storage container in the driveway full of stuff. She also had an affinity for travel. Not only did she travel extensively, but she had a total of twenty-two suitcases. I was surprised by this quantity of luggage, especially since she traveled alone.

Because of her spending habits, she unfortunately found herself in a position where she could no longer afford her home and had to sell it. She had mortgaged the house to the hilt to fuel her love of shopping and to finance her travel habits. Needless to say, she wasn't too happy about having to sell her house and move. On an unconscious level, the stuff was more important to her than the desire to stay in her home.

"It's better to have extra time on your hands and extra money in your pocket than extra stuff in your closet."

—JOSHUA BECKER,

The Minimalist Home: A Room-by-Room Guide to a Decluttered, Refocused Life

I mention the story of Pat and her house because it brings up a very important point. I was brought in to work with Pat to get the property ready to sell. The way that the home looked filled with all the clutter is no way to "sell" a home. Any realtor will tell you that you need to declutter your home so potential buyers don't fixate on the stuff but actually see the house.

When people put their house on the market, they often think it's worth more than it is. They want it to be the most valuable house on the block. However, how you present your home to potential buyers significantly impacts the offers you receive.

When we have lots of clutter, it sends negative signals to potential buyers. A potential buyer can become distracted by all of the stuff in the home, rather than seeing the home's features. They tend to focus on everything they are seeing: the collectibles, the clutter, the clothing, the photos, whatever is around. It also makes it seem as if the home isn't well-maintained, which can lead to low offers or no offers at all.

No one wants to sell their home for less than it's worth, especially when dealing with such significant sums. I was hired by Pat to help her get her house in order and "stage" it so she could get the highest possible amount of money for the sale. When I say "staging," I am referring to the process of making the home presentable to appeal to the most buyers. In this case, it involved decluttering the home and prepacking the items she was taking with her. With Pat, it was not about removing the homeowner's furniture and belongings and replacing them with "staged" furniture. Staging makes the home look and feel its best, signaling to buyers that the home is well-loved and well-maintained, which can attract higher offers. If the potential buyer feels that the home isn't taken care of, then that could lead to lowball offers. Whether buyers are distracted by clutter or assume poor maintenance, both issues make the home harder to sell.

"Messy equals unclean to the subconscious mind."

—CHRISSY HALTON

Clutter often leads to unnecessary spending. Ever wonder why you have so many pairs of scissors, or hammers, or just about anything? How many times have you bought something because you just couldn't find the one you already had? This can happen with any item. Why does this happen though? Usually, it's because the item doesn't have a designated "home."

When an item has a home and is returned to its place after each use, you can easily find it again when needed. Rebuying items multiple times not only adds to the clutter but also impacts your space and your life, not to mention your wallet. How many scissors and hammers does one person really need? I say that in jest, but it's true. I like to call it "repetitive buying."

This is one reason why Buy Nothing groups on Facebook have become all the rage. People often give away items when they find they have multiples of them and realize they no longer need the extras. On a personal note, I love these groups for both gifting and receiving. They are a great way to reuse various items and reduce clutter.

It can be quite entertaining when I work with clients. You never know what will happen and what might come out of their mouths. I always get a kick out of it when we come across a particular item and they say something to the effect of, "Oh, that's where that is," or "I was looking for that the other day;" or my favorite is when they tell me, "Oh, I like that." Guess what though? As I've said before, if that item had a "home," they wouldn't be surprised to find it elsewhere because it would be living in its rightful place. It's basically a rediscovery of something they already own.

This rediscovery not only reduces clutter but also saves money. When items are easily found, you avoid buying duplicates, which cuts down on unnecessary spending. Instead of repeatedly purchasing things you can't find, you can use that money for more important needs or save it for future goals. By giving everything a home and reducing repetitive buying, you streamline your space, save money, and reduce waste. It's a win-win situation for both your wallet and your living space.

When you have clutter, it doesn't seem to stay in one place. Clutter usually grows like a weed and ends up everywhere: your closet, spare drawers, every surface including the floor, you name it. This means that your desk area will most likely be filled with clutter as well; it may be piled with paper on top of more paper. That means that many important documents and papers can become hidden, lost, or misplaced, which can lead to missed deadlines, bills being paid late, late fees incurred, and possibly even penalties. No one, and I mean no one, likes to pay late fees that could have been avoided. They are a total waste of money. This is happening because of the clutter. Imagine for a minute if you had a system in place so that every paper, document, and bill had a place to live. If that was the case, you would easily be able to find each when you needed them, which would prevent documents from getting lost and bills being paid late, thus avoiding those pesky fees. That means more money in your wallet. Woohoo!

One of the biggest pitfalls we see as professional organizers is when clients resort to the use of off-site storage units to hold their excess possessions that won't fit in their homes. Honestly, I am not sure what their intention is for storing all that stuff; I'm not even sure if *they* know why they put it in storage. They just know they aren't ready to let go of the items for good, so they hold onto them, even if it means paying for extra space. This isn't the best idea! The items are rarely ever revisited, but clients continue to pay the storage bill month after month and year after year. Since storage units are so pricey to begin with, the cost of storing the stuff usually doesn't make sense in the long run, especially if you end up keeping the storage unit(s) for a very long time. That monthly storage space rent very quickly adds up.

client story

Let me tell you about my client Stephanie. Stephanie was an elderly woman who I started helping when she got sick and was no longer mobile. We did a little bill paying, a little organizing, whatever was needed. She mentioned to me that she also wanted me to deal with her storage units. She had not just one unit but two of them. She'd had them for over ten years, and now she could barely remember what was in them. *What?* I decided to ask her to take part in a thought experiment so she would understand what it was actually costing her. Keep in mind she had no idea what was being stored in her storage spaces. I asked her how much she was paying monthly for these two units. She couldn't remember exactly, but it was about $125 each. I calculated for her approximately how much she had spent over the last ten years to store who-knows-what.

$125 per month x 2 units = $250 per month x 12 months in each year = $3,000 per year x 10 years = $30,000

Remember I said she'd had them for at least ten years, so that was a minimum of $30,000 to that point to store items that she couldn't even remember. What I do know is that there was probably nothing in those storage units that was worth the cost she had been paying all this time. That is quite typical for most clients. In fact, whatever is being stored can usually be rebought for a much lower price. Once she realized the cost, we very quickly cleared out those units. The sad part is that most of the items ended up being donated because she realized it wasn't stuff she needed, nor did she have space for her stored possessions. She kept very little from those two storage units.

Depending on how full the storage unit is, and how the items are packed and stored, items can often get dirty, dusty, and/or damaged. This obviously decreases the value of any such items and could possibly negate your ability to sell them, if that was your original intention, or even use them. When you finally get to the point and realize that it's time to empty the storage unit, you are going to have to either make multiple trips to and from the storage facility to clear it out or one trip if you have access to a large truck, whether by owning or renting a large truck yourself or by hiring a hauling company to empty the unit for you. Again, this represents money spent unnecessarily on things that probably shouldn't have been stored in the first place.

There isn't anyone I know who wouldn't like an extra $3,000 or $30,000, or whatever the amount is. That truly was a waste of Stephanie's money. I mention this story because I want you to understand that everything indeed has a price. I am sure her intention was never to keep those storage units for as long as she did. But it is common for recollections about what you are storing to fade; it is easy to forget about things when they're not visible from day to day—not to mention the cost to store those items.

* * *

There eventually comes a time when people get to the point where they are fed up with all the clutter they are living with. They either start the process of decluttering on their own, or they hire a professional to help them (money well spent, I might add). When I work with clients during this process, I can't tell you how many times they end up donating things because they realize they no longer need them. Things that once held so much value for them (and I don't just mean monetary value) now have no real meaning because their space and their sanity are much more important. It's ironic to see how the items they wanted and/or thought they needed are things they no longer need to own. The funny thing is that clients often use the term "throw it away" when they are decluttering, and I have to remind them that it is being donated so someone else can get use out of it. For me, nothing gets thrown away unless it is pure trash. I tease my clients by saying that nothing gets thrown away unless it truly is trash because I don't want it to end up in the landfill. As I always say: "I am trying to save the planet one client at a time" (another Robynism).

When you talk about money and spending habits, whether they be wants or needs, the mere act of spending could actually be a real problem for some. When shopping becomes an uncontrollable desire, not only does the home become overrun with stuff from all the shopping expeditions, which causes excess clutter, it could be a sign of something more serious. The person could be suffering from a genuine shopping addiction, otherwise known as a compulsive buying disorder. Yes, this is a real thing! It is a type of behavioral addiction that allows the buyer to feel good and avoid negative feelings such as anxiety and depression. Some may call it retail therapy, but no matter what you call it, it is certainly a waste of money because the person is just buying for the sake of buying.

* * *

As I mentioned in the Space chapter, one of the things I've noticed is that everyone collects something. It starts off innocently enough, often as a hobby. Perhaps you picked up a few themed décor pieces here and there: a couple of rooster items, or ducks, or frogs, and before you know it, it's a full-blown collection of thimbles, Beanie Babies, or Hummels—you get the idea. (I have had real-life clients who own these collections.) The question to ask is when does that collection become clutter? There is absolutely nothing wrong with collections, but there is a fine line between a collection and clutter—especially when you have more than you can display comfortably. When your collection takes over a room and then your home, it might be considered more than a collection. Depending on the quantity involved, some might even call it an obsession. With that obsession comes a high price tag. While the things may be acquired over time, the amount of money spent is the same. No matter how you look at it, one plus one will always be two. Money spent over years is the same amount if you spend it all at once.

Let me tell you about one of the shows that highlighted extreme collections. I remember one episode where the entire home had Christmas items displayed everywhere, in every room...all year long! Not only can a collection take over your home, but it might be considered a waste of money for some. Is it really necessary to spend so much money on collections? Most of us don't have an endless supply of money, and that money could always be spent on other, more important things. The word "boundaries" comes to mind when we talk about collecting. It's fine to have a collection as long as it fits on a shelf or even in a cabinet. It probably shouldn't spill into every space or every room. This is just food for thought.

Many of my clients with children have complained about the number of toys that are given as gifts to their children, usually by their in-laws; if only I had a dollar for every time I've heard this. It doesn't matter if the child needs the toy or even wants it, it's as if the grandparents can't visit without bringing them something. It doesn't even have to be the child's birthday. Not only is this indulgence over-the-top because the child learns to expect a gift every time relatives visit, but it brings more and more stuff into the home. That's my main concern: clients end up with so many toys that it is hard to organize all of them, even in the largest of spaces. Now imagine how challenging that might be if your space is on the compact side; that wouldn't be so easy.

Whether you are the one bringing the toys or the parent of the child receiving the toys, let's try a little experiment. Think back to your own childhood. What do you remember about your grandparents or your favorite relative? Do you remember a particular toy that was given to you, or do you remember a particular outing and how it felt when you got to spend time with that person? I know that for myself, where my grandmother is concerned, even though she lived with us my entire life, I remember the things we did together—the experiences, not the things she gave me. I remember how as a teen I would go with her on the bus to the mall since she never drove, how we played and made forts in my bedroom as a little girl, and how I helped her make her Trinidadian coconut muffins. Even though she died decades ago, these memories fill my heart and make me smile every time I think about them, even as I write this. And guess what? You can't put a dollar amount on any of that. In fact, I can't even recall any toy she ever bought for me. What I find more valuable than toys are experiences with the people kids love. I tell my clients to swap the buying for the doing (another Robynism. I'm just full of them).

"What I know for sure is that when you declutter—whether it's your home, your head, or your heart—it is astounding what will flow into that space that will enrich you, your life, and your family."

PETER WALSH,

Lose the Clutter, Lose the Weight: The Six-Week Total-Life Slim Down

It is always a pleasant surprise when money is actually found amidst the clutter. There have been countless situations when working with clients that we have unearthed money in some form; it could be cash, gift cards, or checks. After all, who wouldn't like to find money they either didn't know they had or had forgotten about? More times than not, it may have been intentionally hidden or just thrown in a drawer or box or something, only to be forgotten. It's surprisingly easy to forget even pleasant things when they're not in view. But unlike misplaced bills that can cause late fees and are never welcome, when money is found, clients are beyond thrilled.

It's not just money that might be discovered, either. It could be an important document they haven't been able to find, a piece of heirloom jewelry, or any number of things. I can't tell you how often I hear clients say, "I was looking for that." While the found item is often something that isn't so important, there are other times when it is something that is extremely important. Either way, it makes the client feel good in the knowledge that the process of decluttering was well worth it.

client story

I was hired by Josie to help her organize her father's home for an upcoming move out of state. He was a self-professed pack rat, so there was quite a bit in his small apartment. In addition to getting all of his things in order, they desperately needed to find the original lease of a tenant they needed to evict. Prior to hiring me, they had searched high and low for this document to no avail. It wasn't until I was hired and we started methodically going through his apartment that it was found.

It goes without saying that the client was elated that the lease was found, since the family would otherwise have had an uphill legal battle if they didn't have it. She was so appreciative; it was as if I had uncovered the Hope diamond or something. To them, it literally was.

The funny thing is everyone thinks their belongings are valuable. In the same way that when someone sells their home, they often think it's worth more than it really is, people think their stuff is more valuable than it is. While the items may have had some value at one time, values can change, sometimes drastically. Think of things you have or your parents had, like collectibles that once held some value but now can only be sold for pennies or given away for free.

Let's look at this in a different way. Many times, valuables are kept in the garage, storage unit, or attic. It could be art, clothing, or ceramic décor items. They are usually not stored in the right way, so over time, clothes can be eaten by moths, books can become moldy, artwork can get chipped or torn, and so on. Plus, depending on how things are kept in the space, they can fall over or other things can fall on them, which can damage the item as well. The point I am making is that something that might at one time have had some value and garnered some money may no longer be worth anything, or at least very little. The value of your 'treasures' can significantly change. Ultimately, you may no longer have the value you thought you possessed were the item to be sold.

The goal should be to not spend money frivolously on things you don't really need or that you can't find. Clients will often try to manage their clutter themselves, but they may not know what to do or even how to get started. They tell me this all the time. If you need help getting your home in order, you could choose to hire a professional organizer. While this does involve spending money, the goal of the organizer is to get your clutter under control by implementing systems that you can follow and maintain; this is money well spent. But it's not as if I'm not biased or anything. The point is that *you can do this*, either by yourself or by hiring a professional.

energy

"Outer order contributes to inner calm."

—GRETCHEN RUBIN

Thus far, in the three previous chapters, we've discussed the phraseology that I often use when working with my clients. We touched on the concepts of time, space, and money. Now it's time to embark on a new adventure: energy. But don't worry, you won't need a Red Bull to keep up. Or maybe you will. Just kidding! The forms of energy we will touch on range from physical energy to metaphysical energy and more. So get ready for the ride.

What is the first thing that springs to mind when you hear the word 'energy'? Think of it in terms of the types of energy that I previously mentioned. Is it the cup of coffee you clutch like a lifeline every morning? Or perhaps it's the Herculean effort it takes to resist the siren call of hitting the snooze button yet again. Maybe it's the sheer determination needed to assemble that flat-pack furniture without uttering a single curse word. Whatever your take, it will certainly be different for each person, and it fits within the realms of energy we'll explore in this chapter. Alongside the more commonplace types of energy, we'll also dive into the world of metaphysical or spiritual energy. Think of it as the cosmic Wi-Fi that connects us all, but without all the annoying buffering. It doesn't matter if you are a skeptic or already in tune with your chakras, this chapter will be an enlightening exploration of the different types of energy that keep us going. So, buckle up and let's get to it!

physical energy

How many times have you looked around your home and realized that you needed to deal with the clutter? A hundred? A thousand? Maybe you're looking at it right now, thinking, "Yup, that's a problem for future me." What would finally prompt you to want to tackle the clutter? Perhaps a surprise visit from your mother-in-law? Or maybe you'd be motivated if you just tripped over that pile of magazines or who knows what else one too many times. More importantly, how do you feel when you think about having to manage the clutter? Are you brimming with excitement at the idea of a clutter-free home, or do you feel a wave of exhaustion at the mere idea of it?

Let's be honest. My guess is that you're probably leaning more toward the dread and drained side of the spectrum. You tell yourself, "I'll do it this weekend." But when the weekend comes, you're just too wiped out from the past week to tackle the mess. After all, watching paint dry seems infinitely more exciting than sorting through the abyss of clutter in your home. Consequently, another declaration of your intent to tackle the clutter is made for the following weekend—and then the same thing happens...again, and so on, and so on. Just like an episode of a sitcom where the punchline is, "Maybe next weekend," the clutter remains.

But why is it so hard to tackle the clutter? You have the best intentions; you genuinely want to get the clutter under control. Somehow you just can't seem to muster the "energy" to start. Why don't you have the energy? The answer is quite simple. It's because the clutter is a black hole of negative energy and it is zapping you and your positive motivation. You would rather do almost anything else, even alphabetize your spice rack, rather than face it. You start off with a positive attitude, determined to conquer the clutter, *wanting* to confront it, but the clutter's negative vibes zap your energy. You then accumulate more stuff, try to confront it again, and around and around you go. It's a vicious cycle.

Let's break this down further. Every time you think about tackling the clutter, you might start like gangbusters with the best of intentions. You get jazzed just picturing a clean, organized space where everything has its place. But as soon as you start, the sheer volume of stuff may quickly overwhelm you. That box of old photos, the pile of unsorted mail, the random knickknacks scattered everywhere—it all adds up, creating a daunting task that feels impossible to complete. Your initial motivation gets buried under the mountain of things to sort through, and before you know it, you're back to square one, thinking, "Maybe next weekend."

Each item you pick up might come with a memory, and then you start reminiscing. And there you go...down the rabbit hole. Ultimately, a decision needs to be made: "Do I keep this? Does it go in the 'donate' pile? What if I need it someday?" All of these questions pop into your head over and over. These seemingly small choices can add up, leading to decision fatigue. Your brain gets tired from constantly having to make choices, and you end up feeling even more drained. It's no wonder that you'd rather do anything else, like binge-watching your favorite show or playing yet another game on your phone, just to avoid the emotional and physical exhaustion that comes with decluttering.

The clutter's negative energy is relentless (more on this later). It doesn't just sit there quietly; it actively drains your mental and physical resources. Every time you walk past it, it's a reminder of an unfinished task, a source of guilt, and a trigger for stress. This constant low-level stress can zap your energy and make it harder to find the motivation to really tackle the clutter or to even start. It's a cycle that feeds on itself: the more clutter you have, the more drained you feel and the less likely you are to deal with it.

* * *

I'm sure you know what it's like to navigate through piles of stuff around your home every single day. It's like living in an obstacle course, and not the fun kind you see on TV with contestants diving into pools of foam and swinging on ropes. Nope, this is the kind where your living room feels like a maze of too much furniture, scattered toys, and precariously balanced stacks of who-knows-what. You're constantly sidestepping around that box of old magazines you've been meaning to recycle, climbing over the laundry mountain that's taken permanent residence on your couch, and maneuvering around the various Legos, toy cars, and baby dolls, hoping one doesn't end up piercing your foot.

This constant need for circumnavigation around the clutter can wear you down physically. At first, you might not even notice the toll it's taking on your body. You just think this is what your daily life is like. But over time, all that bending, lifting, and stepping around things starts to add up. Every time you stoop to pick something up or squeeze past a particularly tight spot, it's like you're engaging in a mini workout. But unlike an actual workout, this one doesn't leave you feeling invigorated or accomplished; it just leaves you feeling drained.

Your muscles start to bear the brunt of this never-ending obstacle course. The constant strain of lifting things that should have been put away ages ago or bending awkwardly to reach something at the back of a crowded shelf slowly chips away at your strength. There's no personal best being set, just the relentless physical demands of navigating through your cluttered environment.

Instead of increased vitality, you end up feeling drained and exhausted. Your body is constantly working harder than it should, and this unrecognized physical exertion zaps your energy. You might find yourself feeling inexplicably tired, wondering why you're so exhausted when you haven't done anything particularly strenuous. The answer lies in the clutter: it's subtly but surely wearing you down. Remember when we talked about the negative energy of clutter? Well, this is quite possibly the manifestation of your cluttered living conditions. On a side note, my clients often tell me they are exhausted after a session of clutter busting, even though they haven't done anything except make decisions.

Not to mention, the clutter doesn't give you any respite. Unlike a workout that has a clear end, your home's clutter is always there, always demanding your physical and mental attention. There's no cooldown period, no time to recover. It's a constant drain on your physical resources. Each time you move around your home, you're reminded of the countless tasks you haven't done and the things you need to pick up, put away, or organize. This perpetual state of low-level physical and mental demand on your attention doesn't just exhaust your muscles; it also wears down your willpower and motivation.

The more clutter you have, the more physical energy you expend just trying to live your life and the less energy you have left to actually tackle the clutter. It's like trying to empty a sinking boat with a leaky bucket. You're always expending effort but never making significant progress. Over time, this can lead to feelings of helplessness and frustration, further sapping your strength and resolve.

So, while it might seem like just a bit of a mess, clutter has a profound impact on your physical well-being. It's not just about the visual chaos; it's about the physical demands it places on you day in and day out. By clearing out the clutter, you're not just creating a more pleasant living space; you're also giving your body a much-needed break. You're allowing yourself to move freely, without the constant physical challenges posed by a cluttered home. In doing so, you're reclaiming your strength and energy, one cleared surface at a time.

One thing you might not have considered is how your sleep may be affected by the clutter. I don't know about you but I look forward to the leisurely end of the day when I get to sprawl across my bed and finally rest—you know that glorious, relaxed state we all crave and yet often struggle to attain. Clutter, it turns out, can be a sneaky saboteur of sound sleep. You might think a messy room is just an eyesore, but it goes much deeper than that. A cluttered space can create a sense of chaos and stress, making it hard for your mind to unwind when you finally hit the hay. Instead of drifting off peacefully, you might find yourself lying awake, staring at the ceiling, tossing back and forth, mentally cataloging all the stuff you need to organize and all the while creating the next day's to-do list in your head.

This mental clutter translates into physical restlessness. Your mind races, jumping from one unfinished task to another, never settling down enough to allow for restful sleep. Instead of counting sheep, you're counting the number of items in that teetering pile of paperwork. And let's not forget the practical aspects of navigating a cluttered bedroom in the dark. Getting up in the middle of the night can turn into a hazardous adventure as you stumble over shoes, stub your toes on boxes, or trip over yesterday's laundry. These little disruptions can jar you awake, making it even harder to fall back asleep.

A clutter-free environment, on the other hand, promotes a calm, peaceful atmosphere conducive to restful sleep. When your bedroom is tidy and organized, your mind can more easily transition from the busyness of the day to the tranquility needed for sleep. The sight of a clean, orderly room can be incredibly soothing, helping to signal to your brain that it's time to relax and let go of the day's stresses. Without the visual and mental noise of clutter, you can more easily drift into a deep, sound sleep, allowing you to wake up feeling refreshed and ready to tackle the day.

mental energy

The mere thought of tackling clutter can be overwhelming; just thinking about what needs to be done, how to do it, and all the decisions that need to be made can completely deplete you of not only your physical energy but also of your mental energy. It's like running a marathon in your mind before you even lift a finger. In order to deal with your clutter and get organized, you need the ability to do so. You need the bandwidth and the mental power to tackle the clutter.

Living with clutter can often lead to low self-esteem, low self-worth, a negative mood, and low energy. It's not just about the clutter itself; it's about the emotional and psychological toll it takes. When your living space is chaotic, it can feel like your life is chaotic, too. This can lead to a perverse cycle where the more clutter you have, the worse you feel, and the worse you feel, the less energy you have to deal with the clutter. It's no wonder that organizing is not something people like to do. In fact, they often dread it. The idea of sorting through all their stuff, making decisions about what to keep and what to get rid of, and finding a place for everything can be so daunting that they'd rather avoid it altogether.

People will even put off calling a professional organizer because they'd rather ignore the fact of how they are living. It's a classic case of out of sight, out of mind—except the clutter isn't really out of sight. It's just easier to pretend it's not there than to face the reality of dealing with it. The thought of inviting someone into their home to witness the chaos can be embarrassing and intimidating. They fear judgment and feel ashamed of their living conditions, so they continue to put it off, hoping that the problem will somehow resolve itself. News flash: it won't.

On the other hand, I happen to be one of those rare folks who reorganizes for fun when they get bored. Crazy, huh? I know it might sound odd to many, but for me, there's something incredibly satisfying about turning chaos into order. It's like a puzzle waiting to be solved, and I love the challenge. I find joy in finding a place for everything, creating systems that make sense, and seeing the transformation from cluttered to clean. It's not just about having a neat space; it's about the peace of mind that comes with it. A well-organized home is a sanctuary, a place where you can relax and recharge without the constant background noise of mess and disorder.

For many people, organizing is the furthest thing from fun. It's a chore, a burden, something to be dreaded and avoided. They might lack the time, the energy, or the motivation to begin, or even the knowledge of how to get started. They might feel overwhelmed by the sheer volume of stuff they need to deal with. They might not know where to begin or how to keep going once they start. That's totally OK. Not everyone has to love organizing, but everyone can definitely benefit from a more organized space.

metaphysical energy

During the nineteenth century, a philosophy called the New Thought movement came to be, based on the belief that thoughts shape reality; essentially, the idea is that a person can influence their life circumstances by changing their mindset and beliefs. This is done through the practice of positive thinking, visualization, affirmations, and utilizing the 'Law of Attraction.' Ernest Holmes is the founder of Religious Science, which was established in 1926 within the New Thought movement with the publication of his book *Science of Mind*.

You are probably scratching your head and wondering what in the world this has to do with organizing and clutter. Well, I'll tell you. Religious Science teaches that everything is energy. When I say everything, I do mean *everything*—yes, absolutely everything, no matter what it is! This includes the chair you may be sitting on, the bed you sleep in, the clothes you wear, the car you drive, the home you live in, and all of the items in your home, as well as...the thoughts you think. All of these things are energy.

Because every single "thing" is energy, that means the clutter is also energy—and not the good kind. I've already mentioned that clutter is negative energy and gives off bad vibes. My hope is that if you didn't know this before, it gives you a different way of looking at things. With the understanding that clutter is "bad" or possesses negative energy, here's my belief: the negative energy of clutter acts as a giant roadblock for positive energy and good things to come into your life. In short, when you live with clutter, it is blocking good things from coming into your life because there is no room for it. This idea may sound a little woo-woo, but trust me, it's true. Furthermore, clutter can hinder your ability to manifest your goals and intentions. In spaces where clutter reigns, your mind struggles to visualize and focus on what you want.

For some of you, this might be a totally new concept, while others might be nodding along, thinking, "Yep, I get it." Either way, understanding how clutter impacts your energy can help you see why it's so important to clear it out.

"Everything is energy... This is not philosophy. This is physics."

—UNKNOWN

the law of attraction

Let's dig a little more deeply into how the negative energy of the clutter relates to your life, and more specifically to the law of attraction. The idea that clutter impacts your energy is intriguing because it connects spiritual ideas with our daily experiences. From a metaphysical standpoint, clutter is not merely a physical accumulation of objects. It holds deeper significance, affecting the energetic flow within a space and within oneself. Consequently, the clutter is disrupting the natural flow in your home. Because of this, the clutter could be affecting you in other areas of your life, potentially in ways you may never have considered.

The law of attraction suggests that like attracts like in terms of energy. Simple, right? If you're surrounded by clutter, which is essentially negative energy, you might inadvertently attract more negative experiences into your life.

The belief that if you focus on what you don't want, that is exactly what you will manifest is an important concept in many modern spiritual paths, including Religious Science. Like attracts like. If you focus on not getting sick, you will usually get a cold or illness; if you focus on being broke, you usually stay that way. This thinking just creates more of the same. So instead, the idea is to focus on what you *do* want as if you already have it. Instead of worrying about getting sick, think of yourself as healthy, and instead of thinking you are broke, instead think that you have a full bank account. In other words, use visualization. Envision what you want as if you already have it.

This concept is actually thousands of years old and has been taught in faiths from Hinduism to Christianity. It actually gained a lot of popularity back in the early 2000s when the book *The Secret* by Rhonda Byrne garnered major media attention after the author's appearance on the *Oprah Winfrey Show*. The book focuses on this very concept. The idea that our thoughts and beliefs shape our reality is a fundamental principle in many religious and spiritual traditions. In Hinduism, for example, the concept of karma emphasizes that our actions and intentions directly influence our future experiences. Christianity often speaks of the power of faith and belief in shaping one's life, with numerous Biblical passages highlighting the importance of a positive and faith-based mindset.

When it comes to clutter, think of it as physical evidence of the mental and emotional clutter we might be carrying around. Our outer environment reflects our inner state. If our homes are cluttered, it might be a sign that our thoughts and beliefs are also cluttered and disorganized. Clearing out physical clutter can be a powerful first step in clearing out mental clutter, making space for positive thoughts and beliefs to take root. By decluttering, you are not just tidying up your space; you are actively engaging in a form of spiritual practice. You are shifting your mindset. You are making a statement to the universe that you are ready to release the old and make room for the new. This act of clearing space can help transform your mindset from one of lack and limitation to one of abundance and possibility. It's not just about the physical act of clearing your space; it's about changing your inner dialogue.

Instead of viewing decluttering as a daunting chore, try to see it as an empowering activity that paves the way for positive change. Embrace the belief that by clearing your space, you are inviting new opportunities and positive energy into your life. This shift in perspective can make the process feel less overwhelming and more motivating. Believe you can do this and you will.

Let me paint a picture that might make it a bit clearer. Imagine your living room is a serene Zen garden, with energy flowing like a gentle stream...that is, until the clutter monster decides to pay a visit! Turmoil ensues, and things are strewn all about the home. Suddenly, that tranquil stream becomes a tumultuous obstacle course, with piles of stuff playing hide-and-seek and your inner peace doing a disappearing act. It made me exhausted just writing this. But hopefully this gives you a visual metaphor so all of this will make sense. Visualization is a key practice in Religious Science.

* * *

Now let's go back to how the effect of the clutter's energy directly relates to the things going on in your life. We've already determined that since the clutter is negative energy, it will attract more of the same. Instead of positive things happening in your life, this shows up as negative things happening in your life.

Let's delve deeper into what that actually looks like and how the clutter can influence various aspects of your life, attracting more negativity into your environment. This can manifest in a number of ways. For example, when your home is filled with clutter, it can lead to feelings of stress, anxiety, and overwhelm. When you are experiencing these feelings, you may well be unmotivated about doing anything, especially when it is something that doesn't come naturally to you, like organizing.

Imagine walking into a room where piles of papers teeter precariously on every surface, laundry spills out of baskets, and random items create a chaotic landscape. It's enough to make anyone feel like they're losing a game of Tetris. This clutter isn't just an eyesore; it actively contributes to your stress levels. The sight of disorganization can trigger a stress response, making you feel anxious and overwhelmed. You might think, "How did it get this bad?" or "Where do I even start?" These thoughts can lead to a downward spiral of negativity. Negative emotions have a way of perpetuating themselves. It's as if your cluttered environment is sending out a distress signal, drawing in more chaos and negativity. The clutter is not just a physical obstacle; it's an energetic one, blocking the flow of positive energy and good vibes that could help lift you out of your funk.

Where you might find opportunities for happiness and peace, the opposite is true when clutter overtakes a space. The negative energy of clutter has an effect on many areas of your life, one that is not positive. Its influence can cause relationships to become strained, it can cause you to feel general dissatisfaction and frustration, and it can be extra difficult to focus on important tasks and goals, thereby hindering your productivity and success. In addition, the mountains of clutter can have a psychological impact, leading to procrastination and a sense of being stuck. It can prevent you from moving forward on important matters, causing delays and missed opportunities.

The negative energy can have a huge impact on your mental and physical well-being.

On the flip side, an organized space fosters positivity, growth, and success. From a metaphysical standpoint, the impact of decluttering goes beyond just making your home look nice—it fundamentally transforms the energy flow within your space and, in essence, within yourself.

When you clear away the clutter, you are actively removing blocks that impede the flow of positive energy. Think of your home as a living entity, with energy circulating in the same way that blood flows through your body. Clutter acts like cholesterol, clogging up the energetic arteries and causing a buildup of stagnant, negative energy. By decluttering, you're essentially performing an energetic cleanse, allowing the positive energy to flow freely once again. Think of it as another way of smudging or cleansing with the smoke of burning sage. This purifying process creates a harmonious environment that can have a profound impact on your overall well-being.

An organized space can significantly uplift your mood. Simply walking into a clean, tidy room can bring a sense of calm and relaxation. Instead of feeling stressed and overwhelmed by piles of stuff, you can enjoy a sense of order and peace. This positive energy can enhance your mental clarity and focus, making it easier to concentrate on your tasks and goals. Your mind, no longer distracted by visual chaos, can operate more efficiently and creatively. An organized space also acts as a magnet for positivity and abundance. By creating order, you are signaling to the universe that you are ready to receive good things. This aligns with the law of attraction, which says that like attracts like. When your environment is organized and harmonious, it helps to raise your vibrational frequency, attracting more positive experiences and opportunities into your life. You become more open to new possibilities, and good fortune seems to find its way to you with greater ease. The good just keeps on coming.

An organized space supports personal growth and success. When you are no longer weighed down by clutter, you have more energy and motivation to pursue your passions and dreams. The clear space around you reflects a clear mind within you, fostering a sense of confidence and empowerment. You are better able to set and achieve your goals since your environment no longer holds you back but instead propels you forward. You feel a renewed sense of purpose and drive as the positive energy in your space inspires and uplifts you.

Can you guess what is also a huge benefit of an organized home? Far less family discord! An organized space can enhance your relationships. It will eliminate bickering amongst family members that once happened due to lost or misplaced items. Not to mention that with the clutter gone, all family members will feel more comfortable in their home. Now everyone can breathe a sigh of relief. When your home is tidy and inviting, it creates a welcoming atmosphere for friends and family. You can entertain guests freely without anxiety about them seeing your mess, and you can fully enjoy their company without distraction. This fosters deeper connections and more meaningful interactions, enriching your social life and emotional well-being.

The clutter becomes a physical representation of the negative energy in your life. By addressing and clearing the clutter, you can begin to break the cycle, making room for positive energy to flow into your life.

> *"A place for everything,*
> *and everything in its place."*
>
> **—MRS. ISABELLA BEETON**

client story

Meet Sally. Sally is what we would call chronically disorganized. She is a kind woman who is overwhelmed by the stuff in her home. Her apartment was so cluttered that she could barely move around. Every inch was filled with items, leaving only narrow paths between rooms. The second bedroom was almost inaccessible, and even the doors were covered with things hanging on both sides. There was much too much furniture and stuff everywhere. This isn't a judgment, just a fact.

We initially started working together because she needed some repairs done in the apartment. It was impossible to reach the area where the work needed to be done because of all the things in the way. Throughout my time working with Sally, as is common when working with clients, I learned more and more about her and her life. I found out that she not only had lifelong challenges with disorganization, but she also had health issues, relationships issues, and job issues.

This situation is quite common, because as we mentioned, the negative energy of the clutter was serving as a block for the positive energy. This was definitely the case for Sally.

"When home feels out of control, no matter what the reason, unsettledness and anxiety can seep in, and then the chaos becomes internal as well as external."

—MYQUILLYN SMITH,

Cozy Minimalist Home: More Style, Less Stuff

Realistically, energy is not something you can see or touch; but it is something you can "feel." Regardless, it is very real. Let me give you an example so you can better understand what I mean. Have you ever walked into a room or office (or anywhere, actually) where something didn't feel right? You couldn't put your finger on it or figure out what was off, but something just felt amiss. You didn't feel comfortable. What you were experiencing was the feeling of negative energy. The space itself was giving off negative energy. It doesn't matter if you were somewhere familiar or with people you know and like, the energy of the space was off-putting.

This is why some people cleanse their new home before moving in or burn incense or sage to energetically cleanse their home when something bad happens. It's all about removing the negative energy. Just as you listen to your inner voice or intuition, you can tune into the energy of a space. When something doesn't feel right, it's often your inner self picking up on subtle energy cues. Trusting those feelings can help you make better decisions about where you spend your time and how you arrange your living or working spaces.

my story

I have been an entrepreneur for many, many years. Most of that time has been spent as a one-woman operation. As you can imagine, there are multiple hats to wear when running a business. I was juggling numerous tasks all at the same time. Needless to say, my desk would get a little messy from time to time. If I'm being honest, it was more than a little messy. Yes, it can even happen to a professional.

Now keep in mind what I said about clutter being negative energy. My desk was full of notepads, bills, and files, etc. When my desk looked like this, resembling the aftermath of a mini tornado, business would slow down. The phone didn't ring as much and new opportunities were fewer. Obviously, this isn't what any entrepreneur wants.

Eventually it would bother me so much that I would hit a wall. I found myself at my wit's end, so I would clear up and organize my desk. Files were returned to their file cabinet, my notes were organized, books returned to the bookcase, and so on. Once again, my desk looked like a place to be productive instead of a war zone. Guess what usually happened next? The phone would start ringing, new business would flow in, and the calendar would fill up with bookings! In clearing the clutter and shifting the negative energy, I allowed the good to reach me.

"The first step in crafting the life you want is to get rid of everything you don't."

—JOSHUA BECKER,

The Minimalist Home: A Room-by-Room Guide to a Decluttered, Refocused Life

There is a huge interconnectedness between energy, manifestation, and clutter. Every manifestation starts with a thought. Basically, you are creating your own reality by the thoughts you think. According to Wayne Dyer, a renowned self-development author and speaker, if we focus on what we really, really don't want, we'll get more of what we really don't want. What he said reminds me of the Spice Girls song "Wannabe," when the lyrics say, "Tell me what you want, what you really, really, want..." Having indulged in a moment of levity, we press on: if you don't want to live with the clutter but place your focus on the negative aspect of the clutter, the clutter will only manifest more clutter into your life. Plain and simple, what we focus on gets energized and increases. In this case, it is the clutter. To bring it all together, clutter or negative energy is created due to a variety of reasons, but it continues to manifest as additional clutter because you continue to focus on the negative aspects of it.

Decluttering isn't just about finding your missing keys (though that's a pretty big win in itself). It's about reclaiming your space, reclaiming your time, and reclaiming your sanity. Plus, who doesn't love the thrill of discovering treasures buried beneath a mountain of junk? It's like a mini archaeological dig, but with fewer ancient artifacts and more forgotten snacks from last Halloween.

By decluttering, you're not just tidying up your physical space; you're conducting a full-on energy makeover. It's like giving your room a spa day—clearing out the cobwebs, dusting off the bad vibes, and inviting in fresh, positive energy. Suddenly, that once-dreary corner becomes a sanctuary for creativity, and your inner feng shui master does a victory dance.

afterword

"You can't reach for anything new if your hands are still full of yesterday's junk."

—LOUISE SMITH

By now, I hope you have come to an understanding of the cost of your clutter. You might even be thinking about how to make some ongoing changes in relation to your clutter.

Additionally, I would imagine that you have concluded which of these—time, space, money, or energy—is the most important factor for you to consider. Maybe it's one of these, or maybe it's more than one. I'm not going to get into the how-to of taming your clutter. There are countless books that can help you with that aspect. You will then see the results firsthand. Hopefully, it will prompt you to make major changes in your life so the clutter doesn't weigh on you any longer.

* * *

I've included some exercises for you to do so that you can get a better understanding of how your clutter is related to each of these areas: time, space, money, and energy. They will help you to pinpoint your most important areas of concern.

time

clutter time audit

- **Exercise:** For a week, track the time you spend dealing with clutter. This includes looking for things, cleaning around clutter, or organizing.

(If a week is too long, then track your time for at least three days.)

- **Reflection:** At the end of the week, total the number of hours spent. Think about what you could have done with that time instead. I'm guessing it is something more fun.

time value of decluttering

- **Exercise:** Choose one small area to declutter, like a drawer or a shelf. Time how long it takes to declutter that space.
- **Reflection:** Based on the time it took to declutter this space, guesstimate how much time you'll save in the future with that space organized. You've just gotten back more time.

space

space mapping

- **Exercise:** Draw a map of a cluttered room (there's no need for great art, a very rough sketch is fine). Highlight areas overtaken by clutter.
- **Reflection:** Envision what that space would look like without the clutter and how you could repurpose the area if needed.

space reclamation

- **Exercise:** Clear out one small area (a corner or a surface) and keep it clutter-free for a week (or for as long as possible).
- **Reflection:** Notice how the clear space affects your perception of the room and your feelings when you enter it.

money

clutter cost calculation

- **Exercise:** List items in a cluttered space and estimate their original cost. Calculate the total.
- **Reflection:** Reflect on how much money is tied up in things you might not use or need. Consider the financial impact of future purchases.

value vs. use

- **Exercise:** Identify items that you have multiples of. Calculate the cost of what you've spent on those extra items.
- **Reflection:** Think about the money spent on those items which were purchased because you couldn't find the first one. Consider selling or donating them.

energy

energy audit

- **Exercise:** Spend fifteen minutes just sitting in a cluttered area and note your energy levels and mood. Then spend fifteen minutes in a decluttered area and do the same.
- **Reflection:** Compare how each environment affects your energy and emotional state.

declutter & recharge

- **Exercise:** Dedicate fifteen to thirty minutes to decluttering a small space. Afterward, note how you feel.
- **Reflection:** Reflect on how motivated you felt to declutter in the first place. Were you excited about doing it or did you dread it? How long did it take for you to even start? Did you procrastinate?

combined reflection

clutter journal

- **Exercise:** Keep a journal for a month, noting any times when you feel overwhelmed, frustrated, or stressed due to clutter. Also, track any positive feelings after decluttering sessions.
- **Reflection:** At the end of the month, review your entries to see patterns and gain insights about how clutter affects various aspects of your life.

clutter inventory

- **Exercise:** Make a comprehensive list of all the clutter-prone areas in your home. Rank them in terms of their impact on your time, space, money, and energy.

- **Reflection:** Prioritize which areas to tackle first based on their impact. Develop a plan to address each area systematically.

affirmations

Consider writing an affirmation that you can recite out loud at least once a day. The more you utilize this affirmation, the more it will become second nature to you, and before you know it, you will tackle the clutter and changes will happen in your life.

Here are a few affirmation examples. Use any of these or write your own.

- I love the sense of peace and calm in my clutter-free home. It fills me with joy and freedom.
- Letting go of clutter feels empowering and liberating.
- Clutter no longer controls me. I control it.
- Getting rid of the clutter gives me more time, space, money, and energy to create the life I desire.

By engaging in these exercises, you'll gain a clearer understanding of how clutter influences different areas of your life, helping you make more informed decisions about decluttering and organizing. In the end, if you need professional assistance, you can find a plethora of available help ranging from in-person visits to virtual organizing to digital courses and coaching. Whatever help you need is available for you. All you need to do is take the first step and make a plan.

references & resources

time

"Lost Something Already Today? Misplaced Items Cost Us Ten Minutes a Day." *Daily Mail*, March 20, 2012. dailymail.co.uk/news/article-2117987/Lost-today-Misplaced-items-cost-minutes-day.html.

"Stress Symptoms: Effects on Your Body and Behavior." Mayo Clinic, August 10, 2023. mayoclinic.org/healthy-lifestyle/stress-management/in-depth/stress-symptoms/art-20050987#:~:text=Stress%20that's%20left%20unchecked%20can,heart%20disease%2C%20obesity%20and%20diabetes.

space

Gromicko, Nick. " 'McMansions' and Energy Inefficiency." International Association of Certified Home Inspectors. nachi.org/mcmansions-energy-inefficiency.htm.

MacVean, Mary. "For Many People, Gathering Possessions Is Just the Stuff of Life." *Los Angeles Times*, March 21, 2014. latimes.com/health/la-xpm-2014-mar-21-la-he-keeping-stuff-20140322-story.html.

U.S. Census Bureau and U.S. Department of Housing and Urban Development. *New Residential Construction*. 2025. census.gov/construction/nrc/pdf/quarterly_starts_completions.pdf.

money

Asymkos, Stephanie. "1 in 4 Americans Have No Retirement Savings—and Those Who Do Aren't Saving Enough." Yahoo Finance, March 31, 2021. yahoo.com/lifestyle/retirement-savings-us-193226292.html.

Harris, Al. "U.S. Self-Storage Industry Statistics." SpareFoot, October 10, 2024. blog.sparefoot.com/blog/self-storage-industry-statistics.

Hartney, Elizabeth. "What Is a Shopping Addiction?" Verywell Mind, December 5, 2023. verywellmind.com/shopping-addiction-4157288.

resources

Institute for Challenging Disorganization. www.challengingdisorganization.org.

National Association of Black Professional Organizers. www.nabpo.org.

National Association of Productivity and Organizing Professionals. www.napo.net.

Professional Organizers in Canada. www.organizersincanada.com.

acknowledgments

My daughter, Kennedy, is the most important person in the world to me. She has always believed in me no matter what, and I mean *always*. She gives me the strength to carry on each and every day. I thank her for being my daily reminder to pursue my dreams regardless of what they are.

The amazing women who raised me, my mother and grandmother, are beaming with pride from above, and I thank them for raising the strong, powerful woman that I have become.

My book coach, Judith Kolberg, was instrumental in helping me write this book. As someone who doesn't particularly enjoy writing but has a lot to say, she was able to guide me in a way so my thoughts would translate to paper, while structuring them in such a way that it made sense.

Everyone needs a cheerleader. Sometimes people see something in you that you don't even see in yourself. Toni Purry is that person for me. A friend from a networking group, her encouragement and belief in me gave me the confidence to finish this book.

about the author

Robyn Reynolds is a certified professional organizer who has helped clients organize their spaces to harmonize their lives since 2008. Her journey to date has been a bit unconventional, from acquiring a degree in fashion merchandising from the Laboratory Institute of Merchandising to an acting career to middle management positions. She finally found her calling when she discovered the world of professional organizing. She never intended on becoming an entrepreneur, it happened completely by accident. In fact, she didn't even know that professional organizing was a thing. It just happened to be her "superpower." Luckily, one day she was reading a magazine and found out about the industry's national association, and just like that, Organize2Harmonize was born. Her company has grown from one woman taking on residential projects to managing multiple projects with teams.

Robyn has been quoted and/or featured in the *Washington Post*, CNN, MSN, the *Huffington Post*, *Real Simple* magazine, Yahoo.com, Today.com, and by numerous other publications as well as podcasts. She has also assisted on the television show *Hoarders*. Having developed a client fanbase, which even includes A-list celebrities, she continues to build and expand her business into digital courses and appearances as a speaker, and now as an author.

In addition, she is a longtime member of the National Association of Productivity and Organizing Professionals (NAPO) and the National Association of Black Professional Organizers (NABPO), a former president of the Board of Certifying Professional Organizers (BCPO), a Golden Circle member, a former board member of the NAPO Los Angeles chapter, and she co-chaired the 2012 Organizing Awards. Her dedication to the industry continues.

Robyn was raised in New York, but now lives in Los Angeles with her daughter. She enjoys a healthy lifestyle, working out every day and focusing on eating for optimum health (although she does have a sweet tooth). She also has a love of traveling and thrifting.

Books That Save Lives came into being in 2024 when the editor and publisher, Brenda Knight, heard directly from readers and authors that certain self-help, grief, psychology books, and journals were providing a lifeline for folks. We live in a stressful world where it is increasingly difficult not to feel overwhelmed, worried, depressed, and downright scared. We intend to offer support for the vulnerable, including people struggling with mental wellness and physical illness as well as people of color, queer and trans adults and teens, immigrants and anyone who needs encouragement and inspiration.

From first responders, military veterans, and retirees to LGBTQ+ teens and to those experiencing the shock of bereavement and loss, our books have saved lives. To us, there is no higher calling.

We would love to hear from you! Our readers are our most important resource; we value your input, suggestions, and ideas.

Please stay in touch with us and follow us at:

https://www.booksthatsavelives.net
https://www.instagram.com/booksthatsavelives/
https://www.facebook.com/people/Books-That-Save-Lives/
https://www.youtube.com/@BooksThatSaveLives

www.ingramcontent.com/pod-product-compliance
Lightning Source LLC
LaVergne TN
LVHW042123160926
848065LV00036B/495